Praise f
40 Rules for Internet

G000141515

"Matthew reminds us that whether
building a business is a process of building relationships, creating value, acting with integrity, and using time-proven strategies for profitability. *40 Rules for Internet Business Success* will walk you through that process — from idea to money in the bank."

— **Dan Miller**, Author of New York Times bestseller
48 Days to the Work You Love
www.48days.com

"If you are prepared to IGNITE your entrepreneurial journey, *40 Rules for Internet Business Success* will inspire you to take massive action and provide you a proven game plan to turn your dream of building your own online business into a reality."

— **John Lee Dumas**, Host of *Entrepreneur on Fire*
www.entrepreneuronfire.com

"Just one of Matthew Paulson's *40 Rules for Internet Business Success* will greatly shorten your journey to your first (or greater) online income. All forty of the rules are proven wisdom from someone who has been there and done it. Read, take action, and you will see results."

— **Jason Van Orden**, Co-Founder of *Internet Business Mastery*
www.internetbusinessmastery.com

"If your business has an Internet component, this book will give you bite-sized, actionable tips and advice to blow it out of the water. Written by an author who's actually done it, Matthew details how he grew, shifted, and pivoted in building his businesses."

— **Emily Chase Smith**, Author of *The Financially Savvy Entrepreneur*
www.emilychasesmith.com

"Matthew is one of the rare breed of business writers who walks the walk. He's practicing, often in real time, what he's preaching. That's why I've been following everything he puts online for years. *40 Rules* provides a unique insight into what it takes to grow a meaningful business from your laptop, and it shows us that having big financial results doesn't need to mean having big offices, staff, meeting schedules, and big managerial headaches."

— **Dan Andrews**, Founder of TropicalMBA and the Dynamite Circle
www.tropicalmba.com

"*40 Rules for Internet Business Success* was written from first-hand experience about what it really takes to build a money-making, online business from scratch. Matthew Paulson shows you exactly how to create a site (or several sites) that will allow you to live the life most people daydream about in their cubicle. Follow his advice, step-by-step, and you'll put yourself in a position to finally breakthrough and earn the money you deserve, working for yourself whenever and wherever you desire."

— **Tim Bourquin**, Co-Founder of After Offers and The Podcast Expo
www.afteroffers.com

"With so much noise (and misinformation) in the world of teaching Internet business, it's refreshing to see actionable advice from an entrepreneur who has been there and done that. Matthew Paulson's *40 Rules for Internet Business Success* provides a proven blueprint that will guide anyone who's willing to do the work and learn along the way to build their own online business."

— **Tim Conley**, Host of the Consulting Fuse Podcast
www.consultingfuse.com

"Matthew isn't one of those people who just writes about success on the Internet; he's actually done it. For that reason, the advice given in his book is time-tested and truly valuable. Matthew has gained important experience as he's built several websites through the years; and these *40 Rules* can help both the budding and experienced entrepreneur gain a better vision for their business."

— **Spencer Haws**, Founder of Niche Pursuits
www.nichepursuits.com

"In *40 Rules for Internet Business Success*, Matthew breaks down the roadmap that led him to become a seven-figure Internet business success story — from making $25/month with advertising to becoming an "Internet millionaire" today! Along the way, you discover that winning the Internet business game isn't complicated, especially when you know the rules. If you want to build a bigger Internet business that nets you more money and pays you a higher salary, read this book."

— **John McIntyre**, Host of the McMethod Email Marketing Podcast
www.themcmethod.com

"*40 Rules for Internet Business Success* is not just a list of 40 items. It is a well-thought-out approach that, if followed closely, will lead to your own Internet business success. Clearly explained points (the rules) followed by action steps move you forward to achieve your goals."

— **Chris Smit**, Co-Host of This Week in Internet Business
www.thisweekinInternetbusiness.com

"Matthew's revenue numbers are more impressive than any income report you'll see in the Internet marketing space. Even better, his business doesn't depend on teaching others how to build an online business—so take his *40 Rules* to heart."

— **Terry Lin**, Host of the Build My Online Store Podcast
www.buildmyonlinestore.com

40 RULES FOR INTERNET BUSINESS SUCCESS

MATTHEW PAULSON

40 Rules for Internet Business Success
Copyright © 2014 by Matthew Paulson. All rights reserved.

No part of this book may be used or reproduced in any manner whatsoever without written permission except in the case of brief quotations embodied in critical articles or reviews. Please do not participate in or encourage piracy of copyrighted materials in violation of the author's rights.

Published by American Consumer News, LLC.
ISBN: 978-0-9905300-0-8
First edition: July 2014.

Cover and layout design: Ellen Jespersen | www.ellenize.com

*To my son Micah, I love you more than anything in the world.
You provide all the inspiration I need to get up early every day
and continue to grow my business.*

*To my wife Karine, thank you for encouraging me
and supporting me in everything I do.
Most importantly, thank you for being my best friend.
I love you.*

"All hard work brings a profit,
but mere talk leads only to poverty.
The wealth of the wise is their crown,
but the folly of fools yields folly."
Proverbs 14:23-24

Contents

Introduction

Having a dream and taking action to achieve that dream are two different things. There are a lot of people who would love to be the entrepreneur with the next big success story and a wildly profitable Internet business. They dream about living life on their own terms and not having to worry about money. They look up to successful entrepreneurs who have come before them, having escaped the 9 to 5, who found work they love doing while still making good money. Unfortunately, very few people who want to build their own online businesses are willing to take the necessary steps to make it happen. Of those who are willing to do the work, many are unsure of how to get started or how to continue their forward and upward momentum when they do. The dream of financial success and a lifestyle redesign remains just that, a dream.

The 40 Rules: Your Game Plan for Success

Fortunately, your dream of developing an Internet business does not have to end in failure like so many others do. You can build a successful Internet business that will allow you to do the work you love, provide for your family, and enable you to live life on your own terms. There are two keys to becoming a successful online entrepreneur: having the will to work hard and having a proven game plan. While I cannot make you put in the long hours essential for a successful business, I can provide a proven plan and rules to follow based on my own experiences so you can build a profitable online business like I have.

The 40 Rules for Internet Business Success is designed for you to understand and implement ideas for your Internet business no matter what your goals are for online success. Whether you are creating an e-commerce store, an information product, a software-as-a-service business, a membership site, a company that provides professional services through the Internet or any kind of bootstrapped start-up, this book will provide wisdom and insight to build your

Internet business the right way from the beginning. Comprised of forty different rules or principles that I have learned over the last eight years, this book takes you from initial thoughts all the way through the strategies that can take your successful business to the next level.

The first section, Developing Yourself, offers healthy rules to live by as you become an online entrepreneur. The second section, Building Your Business, provides experience-based information about constructing your business model and finding the unique aspects of your ideas to get your business up and running. The third section, Running Your Business, contains solid guidance about the day-to-day workings of your business, advice on customer relationships, and recovery from setbacks after your business has launched. The fourth and final section, Growing Your Business, discusses different strategies for marketing and growth once you have gained traction and are running a successful business. And be sure to read my recommended list of books and podcasts for new entrepreneurs and the list of 40 Online Business Ideas to help you discover what business you are uniquely equipped to start. These are found in the appendix at the back of the book.

My Story

I had my first taste of Internet income in 1999. At the time, I was a snot-nosed, fourteen-year-old kid who knew just a little bit too much about computers. I had learned HTML by participating in various online forums that allowed you to use HTML tags in your messages. I built a website around SimCity 2000(R), SimTower(R) and a variety of other simulation games produced by Maxis(R), which is now owned by Electronic Arts(R). I put up information about the game, added my own personal screen-shots, and provided downloads of saved games and cheat utilities. As best as I can remember, I got about 25 page views per day on my website at its peak. I also included a variety of banner ads from a now-defunct network called Safe Audit. For a while, I was making $25.00 per month in ad-revenue from my little website. That was pretty good money for a fourteen-year-old who could not legally hold a job. I tried building a few other websites, trying online money-making schemes like, "get paid to surf" companies, and participating in online rewards programs like MyPoints, too. Eventually I earned enough to purchase my own computer, which cost about $1,000 at the time. Eventually, I got busy with high-school activities and a part-time job at Burger King, and my entrepreneurial spirit took a break until I was in my second year of college.

It was not until early 2007 that I resurfaced online to make money, starting a personal finance blog called *Getting Green* and doing a lot of freelance writing for a company called Associated Content, which was recently purchased by Yahoo. Using Google AdSense and its various affiliate programs, and by selling text-link ads to advertisers, I began generating some income. I later renamed the blog American Consumer News, which became the name of my company when I incorporated in 2008.

In order to capitalize on the direct advertising deals, I built a few other tangentially related websites and developed a small network of personal finance sites by mid-2008. While these sites did okay and generated a fair amount of revenue, around $50,000 per year, I quickly realized the personal finance arena was over-saturated with blogs. I was not going to be the next big name in the category, and since Google's algorithm changes were wreaking havoc on the ability for small blogs to do well in the search rankings, I needed to make some changes.

By early 2009, I was earning about $5,000 per month from my network of websites, but I needed to shift my trajectory if I wanted to continue to grow. I made a slight pivot toward the investing space and created a news website called American Banking and Market News (www.americanbankingnews.com). I was burned out on writing from my past work, so I hired a team of writers to take care of the day-to-day writing responsibilities for the site. American Banking and Market News gained a lot of traction when it was syndicated by places like Google News, Bing News, Topix News Search, and various other news and finance portals. By mid-2010, the site was getting more than 100,000 page views each month.

In early 2011, I decided that it was too risky to continue to rely on advertising revenue alone, so I started a free daily newsletter called ABMN Daily, now called ARN Daily, which became the foundation for my investment newsletter business, Analyst Ratings Network (www.analystratings.net). The newsletter contained a summary of all of the major stock ratings changes that occur in any given day. A few months after starting the newsletter, I created a premium version of the newsletter called ARN Daily Premium where users could receive additional information in their newsletter for $15.00 per month.

In 2012, I launched a piece of investment research software called RatingsDB and made a second daily newsletter available, the Corporate Earnings Report Wire, which provides a summary of corporate earnings announcements. As of mid-2014, there are about 100,000 subscribers to the free newsletters produced by Analyst Ratings Network and about 2,200 customers who subscribe to one or more of Analyst Ratings Network's premium products on a monthly basis.

While I was building up American Banking and Market News and Analyst Ratings Network, I had a day job with a local website development firm that I had taken after graduating from college in 2008. Between my job and my business, I had an overburdened schedule that was not sustainable. I received a wake-up call in September 2012 when my son Micah was born ten-weeks prematurely. My wife and I spent all day, every day with him for more than two months while he was in the NICU.

I knew that I could not continue juggling my full-time job and my Internet business if I was going to be the dad that I wanted to be. My business was doing well and I realized it was time to make the leap and go full-time. The transition went as smoothly as it could and by the time my son was able to come home with us from the NICU, I had quit my day job and went full speed ahead in building my business.

In the middle of 2013, a former coworker, Jason Shea, approached me about joining him in a side-business venture, offering fund-raising software to humane societies and animal shelters. I thought it sounded like a pretty good idea and I knew that he had experience working with animal shelters, so I agreed to partner with him. We spent several months developing an online fund-raising platform from scratch called GoGo Photo Contest (www.gogophotocontest.com). The platform allows animal shelters to run donate-to-vote photo contest fundraisers and has allowed shelters around the country to raise more than $350,000 in its first year of operation.

It has taken eight years to build American Consumer News, LLC into the company that it is today. With American Banking and Market News, Analyst Ratings Network, Lightning Releases, and GoGo Photo Contest, my company now has multiple business units that each generates six-figure revenues on an annual basis. However, it has taken a lot of work and there have been many failures along the way. When I started, there were only a few podcasts, blogs or other resources dedicated to building Internet businesses. I had to learn a lot of lessons the hard way. I wrote this book so that you can benefit from my knowledge and experience. By following the rules outlined in these chapters, you will be able to avoid many of the mistakes I have made on my journey and grow your business faster.

A Call to Action

We live in an era where six-figure and even seven-figure Internet businesses can be built without ever leaving the comfort of your laptop. Thousands of people like you have leveraged their knowledge along with hard work and some incredibly powerful software tools to build their businesses. Many have quit their day jobs to develop their business models full-time and have gained the freedom of setting their own work hours. Others have built healthy side businesses to supplement the income that their day job provides. Building a successful Internet business requires your time, your talents, and your determination, but can be an incredibly rewarding and profitable experience.

The best time to start your own Internet business was five years ago, but the second best time to start your business is today. Think about where you want to be five years from now: do you want to be stuck in the same job that you have today and with the same dream of someday starting your own business? Or, will you look back, satisfied and thankful that you decided to do the hard work to get your business off the ground? Make that decision today and then follow through with a plan to be the entrepreneur that is doing instead of just dreaming. This will mean spending a few years doing what most people will not do so that you can spend the rest of your life doing what most people cannot do. If you read and follow the rules outlined in this book and are willing to work exceptionally hard, perhaps you too will be able to build your own six-figure or even seven-figure, Internet business.

Bonus Audio Interviews

By purchasing this book, you will receive two bonus audio interviews:

Bonus #1: Bootstrapped Business Ideas
In this 40-minute audio interview, I discuss a number of ideas from the second appendix, 40 Online Business Ideas, with Andy Traub of Take Permission Marketing. We discuss the strengths and weaknesses of many of the opportunities in the book and share stories about people who have already leveraged these ideas and turned them into profitable online businesses.

Bonus #2: The Seven Deadly Sins of New Entrepreneurs
In the second bonus audio interview, Andy and I discuss some of the most common mistakes that new entrepreneurs make while building their first business. By being aware of these seven blunders, you will be able to avoid many of the issues that hold first-time entrepreneurs back from launching their first product.

How to Get Your Bonus
In order to get access to these two audio interviews, visit *www.mattpaulson.com/40rulesbonus*. If you have any trouble accessing your book bonuses, feel free to reach out to me at *www.mattpaulson.com/contact*.

Developing Yourself

RULE 1

Know Your Why

Before you make the decision to take the entrepreneurial leap and start your own Internet business, the first question you need to ask yourself is, "Why?" Why are you starting your business? You likely have the option to continue working at your current place of employment and receive a steady paycheck, but you are choosing to put many thousands of hours of blood, sweat, and tears to create a business where there was nothing before. The buck is going to stop with you. You are now going to be responsible for everything: market identification, product development, marketing, sales, operations, customer service, accounting, legal, taxes, and all the other things that come with starting a business. You are going to be the one responsible for putting out every fire that threatens your business and be responsible for making the whole machine run smoothly. Every. Single. Day.

If you want to make it to the top and build a successful business, keep your focus on your "Why".

Building an Internet business from scratch is not easy. Not everyone can do it. When you make the decision to start, you are signing up for months of hard work, sleepless nights and less time spent with your family. You better have good reasons for why you want to give this a shot. You cannot kind-of, sort-of, maybe start a business. If you believe you are ready to make that decision, you need to commit all of your best energy into building and growing. This means remaining head-down for months on end and working hard before you have earned any meaningful revenue. In those moments when you have to choose between staying and working on your business that has not had any traction yet and going out with your friends or family, you need to have your "Why" firmly in place to remind you of the reasons you started your business in the first place.

Your "Why" Shapes Your Business

If you know why you want to start your business, you will be able to answer just about every other important question to shape what your business needs to look like. If your goal is to escape the 9 to 5 to work at home so you can spend more time with your family, you will not want to structure a business that requires you to have an office and a bunch of employees. If you are starting your business because you have to be the master of your own domain, you probably do not want to start a business that will require you to raise venture capital, because you are just going to end up with more bosses.

If you want to have more freedom with your time and schedule, you do not want to build a business that requires you to be on-call for your customers during all hours of the day. If you hope to quit your full-time job and replace it with your Internet business, realistically you will to need to create a business that generates at least as much net profit as your salary paid you last year.

When you have a clear and concise reason for why you want what you set out to achieve, you will have a lens through which you must make every future business decision.

I know my "Why". I have built my businesses because I want to be the master of my own destiny. I want my success to be fully dependent upon my ability to deliver and generate value. I want the ability to generate a six-figure income so I can provide for my family and give generously to the charitable causes that my wife and I care about. I want freedom over my time so I can play with my son every morning, serve in my local church, and have lunch with friends, family, and business acquaintances any day of the week. I want to be able to visit family and go on vacations without having to ask permission from anyone else.

Stay Focused

It took eight long years to get to where I am with my Internet business. I have put in my hours, I have tried and failed and tried again, and now I am living my goals of total freedom over my time while my business continues to provide more than enough income for my family's month-to-month expenses and entertainment. When you have built a successful business that is working for you, you will be able to look back at your journey from where it started. Your decisions and strategies made along the way will seem like no-brainers. Hindsight provides that clarity. But in the beginning, you are at the base of a large mountain that you need to climb. It is easy to wander off the path or give up along the way. If you want to make it to the top and build a successful business, keep your focus on your "Why".

Action Steps:

- » Complete this sentence: "I am starting my business so I can..."
- » List any constraints that you need to be mindful of while building your business.
- » Begin mapping out the other questions that will naturally stem from your "Why" (How? When? What?). Try to answer them. These other questions may change over time, but your "Why" should remain your foundation.

RULE 2

Excuses are the Fuel of Failure

It is always easy to tell which entrepreneurs are going to make it and which ones are never going to get their businesses off the ground. Having worked with a number of new entrepreneurs who have built their Internet businesses over several years, I found that the successful ones will set specific and measurable goals each time we meet. They will accomplish their goals regardless of what is going on in their lives personally or professionally.

The entrepreneurs that run into trouble also set goals, but they frequently miss their deadlines. When I ask why they did not accomplish the set of tasks they told me they want to finish between our meetings, they make excuses about how busy they are. They say things like, "I didn't get a chance to work on my business because I was out of town," and, "I didn't get my list done because I was busy with my family." It is certainly excusable if this only happens once, but there are entrepreneurs who miss their goals week after week. They always have great excuses for why they missed the deadline they set for themselves, but ultimately make little progress developing and implementing their business plans.

As an entrepreneur, you simply do not have the luxury of making excuses. You have to do the work or your business will never get off the ground. When you choose not to work on your business for a few days or a week, understand that you are choosing to keep your business at a standstill. It really does not matter what reason you give to convince yourself that it is okay to take a break from working on your business. Regardless of what your excuses are, nothing will happen until you put in the hard work to make something happen. Since you and your family are the only ones that stand to gain financially from your Internet business, you are only hurting yourself when your work does not get done while you make excuses about it.

If you want to succeed in your Internet business, quit making excuses. Set challenging but achievable weekly goals of what you want to accomplish. Regardless of what else is going on in your life, find the time to do the work to achieve the goals that you set. It does not matter if you have company in town or if you are really busy at your day job, find the time to work on your business. Turn off the TV. Quit playing video games. Skip the outing with your friends. Get your work done.

You will have to make sacrifices with your time while building your business. If creating an Internet business were really easy, everyone would be doing it. While you are building your business, be prepared to put in a lot of extra work. When I was working a full-time job, I often worked through my lunch hours, late in the evenings, on Saturday mornings and Sunday afternoons to get my business off the ground. When your business is successful and after you have quit your day job, you will have more free time to enjoy what you have earned. Until then, put your head down. Do not make excuses. Do whatever you need to do to get your business off the ground.

Action Steps:

- » Set challenging but achievable weekly goals.
- » Build time into your work week to accomplish your goals.
- » Commit to the time and effort it takes to complete your weekly goals regardless of outside factors.

RULE 3

Relationships Trump Knowledge

The people who are the most successful in the business world are not necessarily those who are the smartest or who have the best skill set in their field. Consider how many very intelligent software developers and engineers take salaried jobs that have no upside potential with large corporations. They know a lot more about the technical side of their business than their managers do, but they are making less than their managers. While having specialized knowledge can be helpful in business, the people who really do well are those who can make and maintain their business connections, know the right people, and understand how to leverage the skills and abilities of others. When you take the time to expand your business connections into a wide network of friends and contacts, you will be able to access the wisdom of other business leaders and approach opportunities for yourself that would otherwise be unavailable.

A Real Life Example

Consider the case of Brian Gramm, CEO of Peppermint Energy in Sioux Falls, SD. He freely admits that he has no technical or engineering background, but he was able to start a company that sells solar-powered generators and related products into remote areas of Haiti, Papua New Guinea, the Philippines, and other countries that do not have a reliable electric grid. While Gramm did not have a strong technical foundation, his strength was in his interpersonal communication skills. He had a wide network of connections in the business community from his previous business ventures.

When Gramm saw an opportunity to create portable solar-powered generators for the developing world, he used his business connections to find people that he could hire who had the necessary technical background. He had a friend who connected him to the Governor's Office of Economic Development, a state-wide economic development group in South Dakota, and that group then connected him to graduate-level engineering students at South Dakota State University. The engineering students were able to create a proof of concept of the technology. Gramm then leveraged that proof of concept into a successful KickStarter campaign in 2012, and has since gone on to raise venture capital funding. If Gramm had not taken the time to develop and maintain a network of friends in the business world, it is unlikely that he would have been able to connect with the right people he needed to help get his product off the ground.

How Do You Get Connected?

You might be thinking about your own business connections or lack thereof, and feeling out of the loop without a way in. Remember, every friendship and business acquaintanceship started with an initial meeting. Business relationships are not a, "have and have not" situation. If you do not have the business connections you would like, create them. A great first step is to strategically attend events where the types of people you want to meet will be. Ideally, you will know who will be attending any given event ahead of time if the event is listed on Facebook, EventBrite or Meetup.com.

Strategically attend events where the types of people you want to meet will be.

Identify a few people attending an event that you would like to introduce yourself to and learn a little bit about their industry. Come up with three questions you would love to know about their business, but do not go into the event with prepared notes in-hand. These are conversations, not interviews. People generally love to talk about themselves and their businesses, so quit worrying and ask something open-ended to get your new acquaintance to start talking. After any given event, take the time to connect to the people that you met by finding them on LinkedIn and Twitter. Facebook may also be appropriate in some situations. If they accept your invitation, you will regularly show up on their social feeds and they will be reminded of who you are on a regular basis.

Reaching Out Directly

If events are not your thing, you can also reach out to someone directly. Do not assume that people are automatically going to want to take the time to meet you for lunch or coffee just because you asked, especially if you are reaching out to someone who is a lot more successful than you are. You will need to give them a good reason upfront to agree to meet with you. To do this, find a way to provide value or insight into their business. Do not tell them you want to "pick their brain," because this is equivalent to telling them upfront that the only reason you are meeting with them is so that you can get something from them. When you reach out to someone: show that you have something to contribute.

If you have a mutual friend or acquaintance, ask them to make an introduction on your behalf. If there is a gatekeeper involved such as a secretary who is not forwarding your calls, do whatever you can to befriend the secretary or call at a time when the secretary is not likely to be in the office. You should be persistent about your attempt to create a connection, but do not be annoying about it. Keep in mind that you can still do everything right and not get a chance to talk after several attempts to reach out to that person.

Below is an example of an email I might send out to someone I want to connect with:

Dear John,

My name is Matthew Paulson. I recently read your blog post about pricing strategies for software-as-a-service companies. You had some interesting points. I was wondering if you had ever considered offering a biennial payment option in addition to offering monthly and annual payments. I've personally had good luck with offering two-year subscriptions to my customers.

I'll be in your city in a couple of weeks. If you have time, I'd love to get together and have coffee or lunch to connect and chat about business.

Let me know.

Thanks!
Matt

There are a few basic guidelines that you should always follow concerning business relationships:

- Act friendly and professionally. Do not be that person who only calls when they want something.
- Touch base with your connections regularly to see if you can help them or take time to connect for purely social reasons.
- Listen first. When you are having a conversation with a business contact, do more listening than talking. Do not be that person who cannot stop talking.
- Respond to email and voice mail in a timely manner. Do not be that person that other people have to chase down to get anything done.
- Do not brag about your business success all the time. If you have to tell people, "Look how great I am!" you are probably not that great.
- Be honest. Do not pretend to be more successful than you actually are. Real entrepreneurs will see right through this.

Networking in the World of Internet Business

There are some unique dynamics involved when networking in the world of Internet business, because the people who you should be networking with might be in another state or half way around the world. There are a number of online communities that have sprung up to address this problem, such as the 48 Days Member Community (www.48days.net), the Dynamite Circle (www.dynamitecircle.com), the Fastlane Forum (www.fastlaneforum.com), and the Silver Circle (www.silvercircle.com). You have the opportunity to chat with and learn from other Internet entrepreneurs through these communities. Many of these communities have in-person events that you can attend as well. I have reached out to a number of people through these types of online communities and have made some great business connections as well.

For example, I met a gentleman named Tim Bourquin who had a business in the financial reporting space through one of these networks. After we starting chatting, he told me he had launched an advertising network for financial websites like mine. I gave his new advertising network, After Offers, a try and it became a new revenue stream that generates $7,000 per month in revenue for my company. While you might not be able to get an in-person meeting with someone half-way across the world, you can certainly reach out and see if they would be willing to chat with you for half an hour on a Skype video chat. The connections you make could turn into partnerships and potential for increased revenue.

Finally, as you become knowledgeable as an entrepreneur in your field and are confident discussing the skills you have to offer, consider pitching yourself as a guest on podcasts for the industry that you are in. I have been a guest on a number of Internet business podcasts and have had a number of people reach out to me as a result. Examples include *Entrepreneur on Fire*, *The Lifestyle Business Podcast*, the *Empire Flippers Podcast* and the *SuperFast Business Podcast*.

Action Steps:

» Identify local events for entrepreneurs that you can attend.

» Reach out to one new potential business contact every week.

» Join an online entrepreneur community.

RULE 4

Become a Voracious Consumer of Content

Thomas Stanley, author of the best-selling book, *The Millionaire Next Door*, did a series of interviews with self-made millionaires and found some rather interesting information about their content consumption habits. The self-made millionaires he interviewed tended to not watch much prime time television. They did not know who got kicked off the island or who is sleeping with whom on *Grey's Anatomy*, but they do read one nonfiction book per month, on average. I am certainly not saying that reading a nonfiction book every month will guarantee that you will have entrepreneurial success and become a millionaire. It does however demonstrate the reality that people who build and run successful businesses are life-long learners.

The Value of Life-Long Learning

Entrepreneurs who have had a significant amount of success recognize that there is more going on in their industry and in the wider business world than what they actually know. They know that the world is constantly changing, new information is being updated and ideas are developing that could have significant, tangible impacts upon their businesses. These entrepreneurs accept that there could be critical pieces of information that could change their businesses that they have not learned yet. Unfortunately, people do not know what things they do not know. In order to uncover these pieces of game-changing information, really successful entrepreneurs embark on a life-long journey of continuing education and become better entrepreneurs and more well-rounded people as a result.

Understanding Your Learning Style

There are a lot of different ways that life-long learning can happen.

Do you know how you learn best? You may not be much of a reader and are not interested in committing to reading a nonfiction book every month, but you can listen to business podcasts, read trade magazines, listen to audio books, audit university classes, watch relevant documentary and take online courses through organizations like Udemy (www.udemy.com) and Coursera (www.coursera.com). It is very important to recognize the ways that you learn best and modify your content consumption habits accordingly. If you are an aural learner, consider listening to business podcasts and audio books from services like Audible (www.audible.com) or Audiobooks (www.audiobooks.com). If you are the type who learns by doing, you might benefit from taking hands-on community college courses or professional training workshops in your industry. Of course, if you are the type who likes to read, there are millions of nonfiction books you can choose. The key is to identify how you learn most effectively and consume content using the mediums that suit you the best.

Personally, I do not have a terribly long attention span. I cannot force myself to sit down and read for two hours at a time, but I have learned that I can read in 20-minute chunks as a part of my morning routine every day. I discovered that I can listen to several hours-worth of podcasts and audio books and not get tired of listening. I also do quite well in academic settings, and audit a course from the local seminary or a local university at least once per year. In my journey as a life-long learner, I will read anywhere from 50 to 75 books each year and listen to a couple of dozen different podcasts on a weekly basis.

If you do not practice the habits of a life-long learner yet, get started today. But be realistic, the books that you read and the podcasts that you listen to will not result in immediate breakthroughs for you and your business. But your knowledge base will be solidified and you will gain insight over time. And every now and then, you will find the needle in the haystack and you will uncover something that will change the way you run your business for the better.

For example, my business had been entirely reliant on advertising revenue prior to 2011. Several of the podcasts I listened to then and now stressed that the most valuable asset a business can have is an email list and that the best way to have an Internet business with long-term sustainability is to build an audience of people who you communicate with on a regular basis. Based on this advice, I started offering a daily newsletter on my financial news websites which lead to the creation of Analyst Ratings Network.

The Tension between Learning and Doing

There is a tension at play between learning to become a better entrepreneur and actually growing your business. While it is essential to be a life-long learner if you are going to be a successful entrepreneur, do not convince yourself that reading the latest business book from Seth Godin or Jim Collins counts as working on your business. If you read several business books and subscribe to a dozen business podcasts, but do not actually get around to working on your business, you have not gotten anywhere. Carve out time in your day for both learning and doing. Consumption of educational business content will become the fuel for your entrepreneurial activity, but do not mistake the process of consumption for activity itself.

To view a list of business books and podcasts that I recommend, view Appendix A. "Recommended Books and Podcasts"

Action Steps:

- Determine the type of learning that is most natural to you.
- Commit to reading one nonfiction book per month or subscribing to two or three business podcasts.
- Ask your business connections what they read and recommend.

RULE 5

Don't Leave Your Family Behind

Entrepreneurs tend to be passionate, driven, and highly-motivated people. They are not afraid of hard-work. They are willing to put up with sixty or seventy-hour work weeks for months on end in order to get their businesses off the ground. While this work ethic is admirable, it can be a bad idea to work a crazy amount of hours over an extended period of time.

When you are in the process of building your business, there is a natural tendency to let other things in your life slide. You might miss your son's soccer game or your daughter's dance recital. You might miss your family's sit-down meal time many nights in a row. When your kids or spouse want to spend time with you on the weekends, you might tell them you are too busy with work. When your parents call and ask you to bring the kids over, your excuse is the same: you cannot, because you are too busy. You justify missing a few family events here and there, because after all, you are building your business for them, right?

Don't Sacrifice Family Time

Some entrepreneurs see missing out on family time as a necessary sacrifice. That is not how it has to be. I truly believe there is enough time in any given week to build your business along with having your day job. You just need to be very intentional about how you spend your time. If you spend 40 hours per week at your day job, 56 hours per week sleeping, 10 hours to eat, shower and take care of other bodily functions, you still have 62 hours left to spend with your family, take time for yourself, and work on your business.

When you have a very busy schedule, you need to intentionally invest a few hours of your time in each member of your family each week. That might mean setting aside a specific hour every night after the kids go to bed to talk to your spouse. That might mean planning separate dates or activities with each of your children, if you have children. If you are working sixty or seventy hours per week, you cannot expect to have quality family time by giving your family whatever is left of you at the end of a long work day. Write your family time into your schedule if you have to, but make them a priority.

Your Family Must Be On Board

It is perfectly reasonable and expected that you will work more hours per day and per week than you normally would while your business is in its start-up phase, but you have to make sure that your family is on-board with what you are doing. If you decide it will be necessary for you to work 80 hours per week for the next 6 months, make your objectives and your time commitments clear to your family. If you are married, your spouse definitely needs to be on board with your business. He or she needs to know the timeline of your overtime schedule and when it is projected to end or slow down. If you have children, you need to explain to them, in an age-appropriate manner, why you are starting a business and what that means for them.

Never forget why you are building your business. Most people who start a business on the side have the goal of escaping the 9 to 5 so they can regain control of their time and spend more of it with their families. If your business is consuming all of your time and you are never able to spend quality time with your family, you are defeating the purpose of creating a business. Remember that your business is what you do, not who you are. Do not build your business at the expense of the relationships you have with your family members.

Action Steps:

- Create a realistic work schedule and be intentional about how you spend your time.
- Discuss your work schedule, goals, and timeline with your spouse.
- Set aside time for yourself and each member of your family on your calendar.

RULE 6

Head in One Direction at a Time

It is rare that an entrepreneur has just one business idea. If you are like me, you probably have a file on your computer somewhere that has a list of twenty or thirty possible ideas for different businesses that you could pursue. If you had unlimited time and resources, you could pursue them all. You have to be careful about which business ideas you decide to invest your time and energy into because of the limitations on your resources.

Deciding to work on a business idea just because you have a friend who has an idea and wants to partner with you is not good enough. You should not decide to work on a business idea simply because you imagine it will be easy to execute and will generate a lot of cash. You should only work on the one idea that you are extremely passionate about and believe has the best chance of success.

Build One Business at a Time

A common mistake that new entrepreneurs make is that they work on multiple business ideas at once. They look at entrepreneurs like Rob Walling (www.thenumagroup.com), Patrick McKenzie (www.kalzumeus.com), and Pat Flynn (www.patflynn.me), who have a portfolio of different Internet businesses and want to replicate that success. I am a big believer in the portfolio model of entrepreneurship because you have the diversification that most other entrepreneurs lack, but that does not mean that you should start multiple businesses at the same time just so you can have a portfolio of businesses.

Successful portfolio entrepreneurs generally start with one business idea. Then they put all of their energy and effort into developing it. After the business is established and successful, they create systems of people, processes and technology to run the day-to-day operations of the business so that they do not have to give it undivided attention. They only move onto their next big idea after the day-to-day running of their business has been handed off to someone else and that person is successful in continuing the growth the entrepreneur created. If you are just getting started, you do not have a team of people to help you. Do not expect that you as an individual can do the same amount of work as another entrepreneur who has a team behind him or her.

If you are just getting started in the world of Internet business, start with one idea. If you try to start three or four different ones at once, there is a strong likelihood that you will find yourself with a handful of unfinished businesses that have not gained any traction. Much like driving, you cannot go in four different directions and expect to travel anywhere worth going.

I recommend that you put all of your energy and effort into the one business idea that you believe will succeed. You can get more done when you are focusing on one project and are not distracted by the needs of other businesses. If your best idea falls through, you can always move onto the other ideas that you have. They will still be there waiting for you. If your best idea does work out, you will have a successful business that generates cash flow and you may or may not want to move onto other ideas at that point. You can either decide to see how large you can scale that business or find team members to take over so you can move onto your other ideas. The cash from your first success can fund your next idea.

Heck Yes, or, No

It is almost more difficult to stay focused after you have had some success with your business. Once you have proven yourself to be a successful entrepreneur, you will be the one approached on a regular basis by people who want to partner with you on a project or start a new business with you. You have not only created a business, you have earned the power of choice over future projects. While you should take each request seriously, you have to be very careful about what you agree to do. As an entrepreneur with a now-profitable business, your time is a valuable commodity. You should only say, "yes" to the select partnership opportunities whose potential for success you are most excited about. You need to say no to everything else. Entrepreneur Derek Sivers wrote a popular blog post about this topic, commenting, "When deciding whether to commit to something, if I feel anything less than, 'Wow! That would be amazing! Absolutely! Hell yeah,' then my answer is no. When you say no to most things, you leave room in your life to really throw yourself completely into that rare thing that makes you say, 'Hell Yeah!'"[1] Remember that saying no is a perfectly acceptable answer to any request. You will regret saying yes a lot more than saying no.

Action Steps:

- » Commit to one business idea at a time, and only work on your best idea.
- » Remember: one successful business will make a great addition to your evolving business portfolio. Four failed business attempts will not.
- » Practice saying no. Only commit to ideas that you think are amazing.

[1] Sivers, David. *No more Yes. It's Either HELL YEAH! Or No* (blog). August 26, 2009. <http://sivers.org/hellyeah>

RULE 7

Follow the Supermarket Rule

While you are building your business, you are going to face ethical quandaries. Certainly, you have to follow the law and adhere to any contracts that you may have signed, but the question of what is legal and what is moral are often two different things. You can make moves in business that no one could ever sue you for, but the risk you run in wrecking a business or personal relationship in the process is too high a price to pay. My good friend Deane Barker eloquently referred to this as, "The Supermarket Rule." If you are ever going to do something in business that will sour your relationship in such a way that it causes you to turn and walk when you see that person in the supermarket, do not do it. While succeeding in business is important, you should not build your business at the expense of a series of broken relationships.

Whether your choice is between a friend who has developed a solid business idea you are tempted to copy, legally cutting a business associate out of a deal to get more money for yourself, or deciding to set out on your own and take a team of your former employer's clients with you, providing you have not signed a non-compete agreement, you run the risk of ruining relationships. Keep in mind that these are the same relationships you sought in the building of your business network and need to maintain to continue growing. Those types of self-serving actions at the expense of others tend to spread the fastest in your business network, your industry, your potential partners, employees and clients. It does more than just damage your reputation. It becomes your reputation.

A Short Story

There was a very good public example of breaking, "The Supermarket Rule" a few years back. Leo Laporte had built a network of technology podcasts called the Twit Network, found at www.twit.tv. He frequently had an entrepreneur named Jason Calacanis on his network's lead show: This Week in Tech. Calacanis had been the founder of various companies including: Weblogs Inc. of Engadget, Mahalo, now called Inside.com, and the Launch Conference. Calacanis had created a show called, This Week in Startup, with Laporte's encouragement and blessing independent of the Twit Network. Calacanis then decided to create his own network of podcasts called ThisWeekIn. Many of the shows on the ThisWeekIn network were very similar to those on the Twit Network. After the launch of ThisWeekIn, the relationship between Laporte and Calacanis quickly fell apart. Laporte told Calacanis that he would no longer be invited on the Twit Network. For the years that followed, Laporte and Calacanis would periodically make remarks to defend their side of the story on their respective networks. In 2013, the ThisWeekIn Network disbanded, but as best as anyone can tell, the relationship remains broken. Though Calacanis had no contract with the Twit Network and was legally free to create his own version of the Twit Network, he seriously harmed his reputation and relationship with Laporte in the process.

Don't Break the Supermarket Rule

The best way to answer your questions about your next business move, or decision is to talk to the person or people involved. This may prevent serious issues for you, as well as your business and personal relationships. If you discover that you want to avoid the conversation with that person or group of people, take it as a good sign that you should not move forward. If you do talk and they give you their blessing, you are in the clear to continue with your idea, exactly as both or all of you discussed. Life is too short to leave a trail of broken relationships on the path of your business. Take the high-ground.

Action Steps:

» Don't break "The Supermarket Rule"

RULE 8

Be the Person Everyone Wants to Work For

The way that you treat people will have a major impact on how well you do in business. If you want your team members to give you their best work, make a concerted effort to be the person that everyone wants to work for. This goes beyond deciding not to be a jerk. You have to actively work with and invest in your team members. By making an extra effort to treat your partners and employees well, your team will be more likely to give you their best work and be less likely to jump ship to another company.

I have worked in a couple of different organizations that have not treated their employees well and saw the resulting damage. Employees in these organizations rarely did more than the bare minimum because they did not respect their employer. Employees did not really care if the company succeeded and refused to bring their best ideas to their bosses because they did not think they would listen. There was frequent turnover and these organizations were simply not fun places to work. Because of these experiences, I have committed to treating my employees well.

Guidelines for the Boss When You Are the Boss

The following are my own guidelines that I have developed over the years from my positive and negative experiences as an employee and an employer:

» **Don't micromanage.** If you trust someone enough to hire them to do a job, give them the freedom to get their job done without hovering over them. By providing too much instruction and focusing on inconsequential details, you will waste your team's time and your own.

- **Be conscious of your team's time.** Be reasonable with your time table when asking your team members to manage their deadlines for work with their personal time. Do not ask them to do things you would not do yourself or ask your spouse to do. If they work normal business hours, you should not give them a task on a Friday afternoon with a deadline of Monday morning.

- **Be transparent with your team members.** Your employees should have a complete picture of how your company works and makes money. They should have a clear understanding of how their particular role contributes to the overall mission of the company. You should be open to questions about your company from team members. There is rarely ever a time when keeping secrets from team members helps grow the company. Even if your team member is curious about some of the company's general financial information, it is not likely that they are going to revolt if they know how much money you are making. Which brings me to:

- **Compensate well.** When it comes to paying your team members, do not be cheap. By paying above-average salaries, you will attract great talent and give them a reason to stay with your company for the long term. Having great people on your team will bring in far more value than the added cost of higher salaries. Consider offering end-of-the-year bonuses or profit sharing plans so that your team members can participate in the success of your company. Employees who see how contributing to your company's success is recognized and rewarded will want to continue producing ideas to further the company's gains as well as their own.

- **Surprise your team members.** Every now and then, do something nice for your employees that goes beyond their regular compensation package. Doing so will show your employees how much you value them, especially if you make the gesture personal. I have a virtual assistant who was not able to afford a plane ticket to spend Christmas with his family, so the company bought him a ticket. These gestures do not have to be grand or terribly expensive to be effective. I have sent team members movie tickets, t-shirts, gift cards, and a variety of other small gifts to show them that I care. People appreciate feeling appreciated.

» **Be tough, but fair.** I provide a lot of latitude to team members who get their work done, but I do not have much patience for team members who make a lot of excuses. Set clear expectations and consequences for employees who are having trouble getting their work done and stick to them.

RULE 9

Don't Quit Your Day Job (Too Early)

There are two mistakes that people make when transitioning from their day job to focus on their business full time: quitting too early in the process or holding onto their day job far longer than they should. Some entrepreneurs quit their day job as soon as they start their business. They jump off a cliff and hope they can build a parachute as they fall. They believe working without a safety net will push them to succeed. This is not a winning game plan.

When your fledgling business has to generate sufficient cash flow to pay for your family's living expenses right away, you tend to get desperate and take deals that may end up hurting your potential for success. Deals that are significantly discounted or have onerous terms, business from a problem customer, or work you accept only because it pays the bills can all cause you to lose focus on your goals.

You might also be inclined to grow your business too quickly and scale your company before you have a proven business model. This can be dangerous because any fatal flaws in your business model will be magnified.

On the other side, there are people who hang on to their day jobs far longer than they should because their steady paycheck is their safety net. Should their business fail, they still have income. This sounds nice for the risk-adverse, but there is a large opportunity cost to keeping your day job. Your best energy and work efforts are directed towards growing your employer's business, not your own. Your business will get short-changed and you will probably not pursue as many opportunities to improve and expand as you would if you were fully dedicated to your business.

Another reason people keep their day jobs is to hold onto their employee health insurance and other benefits. While acquiring an individual health insurance policy was a significant roadblock to self-employment in the past, this is no longer the case. The Affordable Care Act prevents insurers from rejecting your application because of pre-existing conditions. You can shop for a policy through your state insurance exchange or through an independent insurance agent. If you are self-employed and are paying for your own health insurance, you may be able to deduct what you pay monthly for health insurance from your taxes. Depending on your income, you may also qualify for a federal subsidy towards the cost of your insurance policy. Paying for a health insurance policy on a monthly basis can still be very expensive, but it is not an insurmountable challenge that would prevent you from going full-time with your business.

I was in the camp that held onto their day job for too long. After I graduated from college, I took a job working for a local website design firm in mid-2008. I enjoyed the work, completed all of the projects I was assigned, and thought I had given myself plenty of time to build my business at home as well. Two years later, my online business was generating as much revenue as my day job.

However, when my son was born prematurely in September 2012, I realized I did not have the time to work two full-time jobs and be a full-time dad, so I made plans to transition from my day job to full-time self-employment. I gave my employer four weeks' notice and by November 2012 I was fully-focused on growing my business. With a newborn in the house, there was a possibility that my business would suffer, but just the opposite happened. Since I could now put all of my energy toward my business, I was able to pursue all of the ideas that had been floating in the back of my mind. Within six months of quitting my day job, my business's monthly income doubled and has been growing at a steady clip since then.

The question of when exactly you should jump ship and focus solely on your business is not easy to answer because no one knows what the future holds. If you could see your future income statements, the decision would be much easier. If you knew your business was going to grow significantly during the next few years, you would quit sooner rather than later. On the other hand, if you knew that your company's revenue was going to tank, you would hold on to your day job for dear life. Unfortunately, you cannot be certain about your company's performance in the months and years after you quit your day job, so you have to act on the best information you have available.

I recommend you quit your day job when your business has generated more net profit than your salary for three consecutive months and your projected net income shows there is a reasonably good chance that trend will continue. While working toward this goal, I also recommend living only on your salary and using the net profit from your business to pay off debt or build an emergency fund. This will put you in a much better financial position when it is time to quit your day job and will prevent you from building an expensive lifestyle that requires the income from both your day job and your business.

Action Steps:

» Identify how much revenue your business will need to generate before you can quit your day job.

» Use the income from your side business to pay off debt and build an emergency fund for your family.

» Quit only when net profits are greater than your salary for three consecutive months.

RULE 10

Prepare for Failure: Plan for Success

When you are building your business, you need to prepare for both failure and success. By planning for the possible failures of your business venture, you will have a parachute to help break your fall on the way down. You may think your business has great prospects and see nothing but sunshine and rainbows in the near future for your company, but the reality is that nearly half of new businesses fail within the first five years and two-thirds of new businesses will fail within the first ten. These are not impossible odds, but they are an indicator that your first business venture will probably not be your last. Dealing with instances of major failure in your business along the way will change you and how you look at your business model.

Financially Preparing for Failure

To effectively plan for failure, you need to make sure that you are both emotionally and financially prepared for its possibility. Preparing for failure in terms of your finances is the easy part. It makes sense to reduce the amount of debt you carry and build as large a cushion as possible in savings. Dave Ramsey and other financial personalities tend to recommend building a three-to-six month emergency fund. Thomas Stanley, author of *The Millionaire Next Door*, reported that some millionaires that he interviewed had built up two year's worth of emergency savings or more. That way, they could weather the total failure of their business and have time to get something else started. Do not panic if you do not have a healthy emergency fund in place, but know that if you are already self-employed or preparing to go full-time with your business in the next year, now is the time to start putting some cash away for a rainy day.

The other way to make sure you are okay financially when the inevitable failure does come is to have a good, "Plan B" for how you can generate some cash. I maintain friendly relationships with several different website design agencies in the city that I live in. I know that if my business were to suffer a total failure, I would likely be able to get a job with them or at least do some consulting work for them to provide a stream of income for a period of time. I also know that I could do some freelance writing, or scrounge up some other freelance development work to generate an income in a worst case scenario.

Another option would be to create secondary revenue streams that will still provide some amount of income even if your primary business fails. For example, I started a side business last summer with a couple of friends of mine that generates $1,000-$2,000 per month in additional income for my family. My partners run the day-to-day operations of the business, but I have an equity share in the company in exchange for doing some of the programming and administrative work up-front and helping with marketing and finance when the need arises.

Emotionally Preparing for Failure

Preparing emotionally for failure is a much more difficult task. As an entrepreneur, you are very passionate about your business ideas and you think of them as a member of your own family. There is almost a grieving process that you go through when you lose part or all of your business, especially the first time. I do not have a formula or plan to recover from those emotions when they do come, but knowing that failure is always a realistic possibility and giving yourself permission to grieve over the loss of your business for a specific period of time is a healthy thing. It is always good to have a list of new business ideas in a notebook or on your laptop you can look at to determine future possibilities when you are in the midst of failure.

Planning for Success

Conversely, you should also plan for the possibility of your business becoming a wild success. What happens if the demand for your business's product or service is much greater than you thought it would be? Will you be able to meet that demand? If your business is solely reliant on a particular skill that you have to offer, a service you provide, or a product you build, your business is going to hit a ceiling in revenue growth when you run out of time. While your business may only start off with you as the sole employee, you need to start thinking about how your business might be structured if it were operating at a significant scale.

Start thinking about how you can grow your business beyond yourself. Who should you hire to help run your business? What skills, education, and personality would they need to work well with you to grow your company? What would your organizational chart look like? What additional equipment, technology or office space will you need? How will your business look when it is much larger than it is now? What does your role look like when your business is ten times its current size? If you can answer these questions, you are on your way to being equipped for the possibility that your business succeeds beyond your expectations.

Action Steps:

» Build an emergency fund of three-to-six month's salary to pay bills as you weather downturns in your business.

» Have your, "Plan B" to earn income if your business stops generating revenue.

» Create an organizational chart for what your business looks like when it is operating at scale.

Building Your Business

RULE 11

Market Selection is a Make or Break Decision

When you first decide that you want to build an Internet business, you will have several possible ideas about products or services that you could create, as well as potential markets you could target. Think of a market as a group of people in a specific category who have similar problems and needs. Selecting your target market is perhaps the most important early decision to consider when starting your business. If you pick the right market, you will have an easier time identifying the problems that your target audience faces. You will have scores of customers ready to purchase your product or service after you do some basic marketing. If you pick the wrong market, you will face an uphill battle every step of the way.

Select a Target Audience in a Growing Market

By selecting an industry to target that is growing substantially in size, you will have an easier time attracting new customers. The easiest customers to acquire are those who have not already made a purchasing decision for the product or service that you offer. But you have to find them first, and figure out where they congregate online. In order to identify your target audience, you must first decide who your ideal potential customer is. How old is your typical customer? What do they do for a living? What gender are they? Are they married? Where do they live? What are their interests? What problems do they face? How much money do they spend online? Create a range for your target demographic that is not too large and overreaching or so small that you limit your customer base.

Once you have identified a target audience for your product, be careful not to build a new product or service in declining industries. You would never build a product or a service that targets video rental stores in 2014. Instead, you would plant your flag in fast growing markets like smartphones and portable devices. As the saying goes, a rising tide raises all ships. When you are working in a growing market, your company and every other company in that industry will benefit from the growth. When you are evaluating different industries you might target, evaluate the industry growth trends to make sure that you are not signing up to compete in a shrinking industry.

Don't Try to Be Everything to Everyone

Select a small subset of a large industry and serve that subset well. There is a company in the city where I live called Docutap, (www.docutap.com). They set out to build better Electronic Medical Records or EMR software in the early 2000's. Instead of trying to offer their EMR software to every known category of medical provider, they decided to exclusively target urgent care clinics. They were able to target their EMR software to the specific needs of urgent care centers and have had great success as a result. While the urgent care industry did not exist 30 years ago, there are now more than 9,000 urgent care clinics in the United States. Docutap skillfully selected a small, but fast-growing subset of the health care industry and served them very well. While you may not be thinking about creating a software company that has 200 employees, the lesson still applies.

Focus your efforts to better serve your target group. For example, do not create an online community for athletes. Instead create an online community for barefoot runners in cold climates. Do not create a business that provides editing services to authors. Create a business that provides editing services to self-published nonfiction authors who write about business and entrepreneurship. When you try to create a business that serves everyone, you tend to build a service that serves no one.

Sell to People Who Are Willing To Buy

Find a target audience who has money and is willing to buy the products and services you offer. Ideally, you will find a group of people who already buy a product or service on a regular basis. That way, you can just do the work needed to convince them to buy from you the next time they are going to purchase that product or service. Selling to a cash-strapped target audience or an audience who is used to getting stuff for free is not serving your best interests. For example, you are probably not going to have much luck selling to college students. While you may have the best product or service in the world for them, you are not going to be able to stay in business because they will not have the extra money to spend on you.

You also want to be careful not to select a brand new business idea that no one is doing. If you have no competitors, it could be a sign that the market you want to enter into is not a valuable market to be in. When you start a new business category from scratch, you have to inform your potential customers about your product or service, persuade them through advertising that they need your product or service, and then convince them to trust you. This is an uphill battle you do not need to fight when you are first starting out on your own. Initially, it is easier to "plug in" to an existing market of customers who are already buying from someone else.

When I built my press release distribution service, Lightning Releases, I found a target audience who had money and who were currently buying press release distribution services from other companies on a regular basis. I did not have to convince people to buy press release distribution services because they already knew that they wanted to send their press releases out to a wide network of media outlets. I only had to create a value proposition for my service that made my target audience want to use my company instead of a competitor the next time they had a press release to send out. Lightning Releases was able to carve out a small portion of the press release distribution market by offering distribution services to authors, small non-profits, and private companies that did not want to spend $400 to have each press release sent out by one of the big-name firms. By offering a wide distribution network at an affordable price point, Lightning Releases was able to sell approximately 1,500 releases at $100 each in its first year of operation.

Select a Market You Know and Understand

Finally, build a product or a service for a market where you have background knowledge and possibly experience. You could leverage knowledge you have gained from one of your hobbies or a prior place of employment. Maybe you already know several people in the market where you want to start your business and can ask them for feedback and advice. The key is to have a working knowledge of a particular market before you try to serve that market. When you pick out a market that you know nothing about, you make yourself prone to a lot of rookie mistakes. You may misread the market and build a product or a service that no one actually wants. You may get your pricing entirely wrong. There may already be a solution for the problem you are trying to solve or your target audience may not see the problem you perceive as a problem at all. By having a working knowledge of your potential audience and market, you are prepared to sell more successfully to consumers who are willing to buy.

Action Steps:

- Make a list of all the markets you understand or have experience with that have the potential to be consumers of your product or service.
- Identify which of those markets are growing and which are shrinking.
- Create a list of potential subsets of each growing market on your list that you can target.

RULE 12

Don't Become a Copycat of Someone Else's Business Model

It can be very tempting to become a follower of an Internet business personality and try to replicate their success by doing what they did when you are just starting out. These personalities include people like Pat Flynn of *Smart Passive Income* (www.smartpassiveincome.com), Dan Andrews of *TropicalMBA* (www.tropicalmba.com), Jeremy Frandsen and Jason Van Orden of *Internet Business Mastery* (www.Internetbusinessmastery.com) and John Lee Dumas of *Entrepreneur on Fire* (www.entrepreneuronfire.com). They have had significant success in their online businesses and have popular blogs, podcasts and online communities of like-minded people who are or want to be entrepreneurs. It is easy for new entrepreneurs to imagine that if they just started a blog, a podcast, a series of small income-generating websites, and release a monthly income report, they could be the next Pat Flynn. Unfortunately, it does not work like that.

What Worked Then Won't Work Now

You cannot expect to have any meaningful success by copying exactly what Pat Flynn or Dan Andrews did to build their brands five years ago. The Internet has changed a lot during the last half-decade and what made those entrepreneurs special in 2009 is now commonplace in 2014. They differentiated themselves by building high-quality podcasts during a period where there were a relatively small number of business podcasts on iTunes. Now, there are hundreds of podcasts about doing business online. Having a podcast no longer makes you different or better than anyone else. The same is true for courses that teach you how to build Internet businesses. Following an online course and expecting to have a meaningful amount of success is not realistic. Your business model will not be much different than the others who have taken the same course that you did. You need to find something new that not everyone else is doing to stand out from the crowd. Fortunately, this book is not a how-to guide to create a business that is exactly like mine or anyone else's. Instead, these 40 rules provide a framework for you to build a business based off the potential that will develop from your strengths and interests.

When I started my investment newsletter business, Analyst Ratings Network, in 2011, everyone thought that email newsletters were dead. At the time, the trend in financial news was to build big, all-inclusive news and research websites that published dozens of articles each day and had a wide variety of investment research tools for investors to use. I set myself apart from the rest of the financial news community by reporting on one thing, stock ratings, better than anyone else and by publishing the data in a very convenient format, a daily email newsletter. Because I have been able to differentiate myself successfully, I have been able to grow that business to more than 100,000 subscribers in just over three years.

Your Business Must Fit Your Personality

Copying the personality of the Internet celebrity whose business you are trying to replicate is like walking in someone else's shoes. It is uncomfortable and hard to do because is not the right fit. Your strengths, skills, and personality are likely different from that celebrity and his or her business model you are hoping to emulate. Even if you were to put in the hard work and hours to create a daily podcast like *Entrepreneur on Fire*, your rate of success will differ from John Lee Dumas's success because you cannot replicate his personality, his work ethic, or his celebrity status. Build your business: showcase the talents you have with the hard work you commit to doing to create your own success.

Showcase the talents you have with the hard work you commit to doing.

My investment newsletter business fits my skills and personality: it effectively leverages my software development skills and my ability to collect, organize and distribute financial data. By focusing in this way, I can avoid the things that I am not particularly good at. I am a type-B personality, so I have built a business that does not require me to be around people all day. Also, I am not a particularly talented public speaker or the type of person who wants fame, so you will not see my name as a part of the brand for any of my online businesses and I tend not to show up at conferences as a guest speaker. It is worth spending a lot of time thinking about what you are good at, and what you are better at than most people. Consider reading the book *StrengthsFinder 2.0* and completing the associated online assessment. The key is to build a business that connects as many of your strengths as possible and requires as few of your weaknesses as possible.

Action Steps:

- Identify your key differentiator. How will your business be different?
- Be current, focused, and aware of your strengths and weaknesses in your skills set and personality.
- Consider completing the StrengthsFinder 2.0 Assessment.

RULE 13

Have a Business Model, Not a Business Plan

If you were to spend time and money earning a business degree, you may be required to create a fifty-page business plan that describes every minor detail of your theoretical business before you graduate. Universities cannot make starting a business a requirement, so they will ask you to describe your theoretical business in great detail instead. Creating a lengthy business plan may be a useful academic exercise, but it is not useful when trying to achieve any meaningful business goals in the real world.

At best, a lengthy business plan is an unproven theory about how your business could work. Lengthy business plans rarely survive their first contact with actual customers. As you become more familiar with your market and start working on your product, significant portions of your business plan may change in order to accommodate the realities of your target market. Do not spend a large amount of time writing down the specific details of a business plan in lieu of actually working on your business.

Building an Audience Is Not Building a Business

While some people put too much focus on creating a business plan before starting, others make the mistake of having no plan at all. These people will start writing a blog or publishing a podcast without any real plan to create revenue. Blogs and podcasts are best used as marketing tools that will help attract people to your message, but having an audience does not mean that you have a business. Having an audience just means that you can start a conversation online and someone will actually listen to you. In order to have a business, you need to have products and services to sell to your audience and a marketing strategy to get them to buy so you can generate revenue.

If your goal is to create a profitable company, you need to be selling something to somebody. Do not mistake having an audience for having a business.

Creating Your Business Model

In lieu of creating an extended business plan or not creating a plan at all, I recommend creating a one-to-two page document outlining the basic components of your business model. This will help you make sure that you have all of your bases covered and will help you process how you communicate what your business does to others. In this document, you should:

- » Describe your potential target markets.
- » Describe your product or service with attention to its features, benefits, and customer solutions.
- » Discuss product marketing and initial marketing channels you plan to use to acquire customers.
- » Outline your delivery process: which people, skills, equipment and software do you need to provide your product or service to your customer?
- » Include a rough estimate of your company's finances based on product pricing and estimated expenses in the first year.
- » Know how many customers you will need to have to break even.

Completing this short document will ensure that you have a starting point for every major component of your business.

Action Steps:

- » Identify your current mode: are you building a business model or just an online presence and audience?
- » Create your business model document.
- » Make sure the components of your business model are clearly articulated: target market, product or service, marketing strategy, pricing, and methods of delivery.

RULE 14

Let Your Customers Develop Your Product

Entrepreneurs commonly make the mistake of assuming that they know what their clients' needs are and build out their product or service before ever actually talking to a potential customer. If you finalize your product before talking to your customers, there is a good chance that you will build something that they do not want or need. Your product may not solve any of their actual problems. Keep in mind that your ideas about your product are valuable, but your customers know their wants, needs and frustrations better than anyone. It is important that you take the time to listen and get feedback from people in your target market before diving into product development.

> *Take the time to listen and get feedback from people in your target market.*

Find a Problem to Solve

The key to building a great product is to identify a major problem, pain, or frustration that your target market has and to identify or create a solution that will solve that problem. Customers, especially business customers, will happily pay money for products that address significant problems they currently struggle with if it saves them time or money, or both. If the people in your target market have a headache, they will gladly buy Tylenol(R) from you to make their headache go away. Your potential customers will be more than happy to tell you about the problems and frustrations they have.

For example, when I was launching the premium version of ARN Daily Premium, many of my potential customers told me that they were frustrated because there were no single comprehensive resources that had a full summary of all of the stock research notes that brokers publish on a daily basis. As a result, one of the initial product goals for ARN Daily Premium was to provide the most comprehensive coverage of stock research reports. By having a clear understanding of what problems your customers face, you will be able to build a product that effectively addresses their issues in order to keep them coming back as your customer.

Talk to Potential Customers

I recommend that you meet with at least three people who could potentially be consumers of your product. If you are building a product that helps dental offices with marketing strategy, go out and interview three different dentists. Start with a list of five or six people you want to interview, knowing that a few of them will likely turn down your request. When you are planning your meeting, tell them that you are developing a product for their industry and you would like their input. Do not try to sell them your product when you first meet with them. At this phase, you are only trying to gather information. Make sure to take notes during your meeting so that you remember what each of your interviewees said.

I recommend asking these questions to the three people that you interview in your target market:

- » What are the most pressing problems you have?
- » What are the most frustrating aspects of your business?
- » What are you doing now to address the issues that you mentioned?
- » What are the advantages and disadvantages of your current solution?
- » What potential alternative solutions could more effectively address your issues?

If your interview is going well, you can feel out the following questions to help you identify potential marketing channels. Again, do not try to sell your product or service here.

- » How do you find out new information about your industry?
- » Are you a part of any professional groups?
- » Do you subscribe to any trade magazines or visit any industry websites on a regular basis?
- » Do you attend any conferences or trade shows?
- » Who makes the purchasing decisions in your organization?

After asking the other questions first, tell them about your current idea for your product or service. Ask them if it would solve any problems for them. Ask them how they would improve your product to better fit their needs. Pay attention to their reaction to your ideas and write down any suggestions they may give you that would fit their needs. Be sure to thank them for their time.

Find Online Professional Groups for Additional Feedback

If you are building a product for businesses or any type of professional, consider using LinkedIn groups as a way to get additional feedback about your product or service. I have a friend who is building a marketing service for massage therapists. He posed a couple of open questions on the American Massage Therapy Association LinkedIn group and received fifteen responses to his questions in 48 hours. While online professional groups are not a replacement for meeting with your customers in person, they can provide confirmation about what you have learned in your interviews or generate better questions to ask your specific target market.

Follow Up

After you have conducted your interviews and have a better idea of what kind of product or service you should create, follow up with the people that you interviewed at a later date. Tell them about the product or service you are building and ask whether or not it would solve their current problems. If you plan on pitching your product when you follow up with them, ask them to commit to buying when you meet with them and get their first payment if possible. If they tell you that do not want to buy your product, be sure to ask for the reasons why. This could be one of the most helpful pieces of feedback that you get.

Action Steps:

- Interview three potential customers in person.
- Confirm what you have learned from your interviews through online discussions.
- Follow up with potential customers to tell them about your product and receive feedback if you give your sales pitch.

RULE 15

Be Unique

After you have identified your target market and the type of product or service that you want to sell, your next step is to determine what will make you different from your competitors. You need to develop your unique selling proposition (USP), which answers the question, "Why would my customers buy from me instead of my competitors?" You have to determine what unique features or benefits your company can offer to your customers that your competitors cannot. Your unique selling proposition should make a promise to your customers about what they should expect from your business and its products and services. Your USP should be inseparable from your brand in the mind of your customer. Your USP will create a framework for every business decision that you make moving forward.

Here are some successful examples of unique selling propositions in corporate history:

» Domino's Pizza: "You get fresh, hot pizza delivered to your door in 30 minutes or less—or it's free."
» FedEx: "When your package absolutely, positively has to get there overnight."
» Kiva: "Loans that Change Lives"
» Southwest Airlines: "We are the low-fare airline."
» TOMS Shoes: "With every product you purchase, TOMS will help a person in need."

Your unique selling proposition does not have to fit into a one-sentence catch phrase, but it should define who you are as a business. Amazon's USP is its commitment to creating the best online shopping experience that currently exists. Zappos' USP is its offer of over-the-top customer service. Your USP can be just about anything that your customers care enough about that differentiates you from your competitors.

The best way to develop your USP is by talking to your potential customers and listening to what they do not like about the industry space that you are in. For example, if you were opening up a lawn care service, you might hear from your potential customers that it is almost impossible to get lawn care service companies to show up when they say they are going to show up. You could turn that frustration into your unique selling proposition by guaranteeing that you will show up within an hour of the specified time that you stated.

Don't Compete on Price

There is one thing that should not be your unique selling proposition: price. Your USP should never just be that you are cheaper than your competitors. Having a war with other companies in your market space, to determine who can charge the lowest price, is a great way to ensure that nobody in your market has a profitable business. Instead of trying to be the cheapest company in your space, provide your customers more value or unique benefits that your competitors cannot offer. Price is not the key determining factor that consumers use to make purchasing decisions. If it were, everyone would be shopping at Dollar General and Dollar Tree. People are willing to pay more for your product if they see the value in it. Apple's smartphones and MP3 players are some of the highest priced in the market, but consumers buy them every day because they see value in the products that Apple offers.

Internet Businesses Have USPs, Too

Unique selling propositions are not just something that publicly-traded companies do. Small Internet businesses need to create and utilize them as well. Pat Flynn (www.patflynn.me) created a name for himself by being absolutely transparent with his readers and sharing how much income he made every month. Steve Kamb created a wildly successful online fitness community by catering specifically for nerds (www.nerdfitness.com). Chris Ducker was able to set himself apart from other Internet business gurus by focusing exclusively on teaching how to leverage virtual assistance (www.chrisducker.com). Jaime Tardy was able to set her show apart from other interview podcasts by exclusively interviewing millionaires (www.eventualmillionaire.com). There is a unique selling proposition behind every great online entrepreneur. Look for what your competitors are lacking, what your customers are frustrated with in your industry, or what you could combine effectively to meet customer needs in a unique way.

When I started Analyst Ratings Network in 2011, I had heard from a number of frustrated individual investors who were tired of not being able to access fast and reliable financial data. My readers also told me that the data analysis they saw was sometimes biased, coming from financial authors who owned the stocks that they wrote about, and they were not impressed. There are expensive services from Bloomberg and Reuters that provide professional investors up-to-the-minute financial information, but these services are out of reach for retail investors. Based on this feedback, my unique selling proposition for Analyst Ratings Network has become providing real-time financial data in a convenient format. I am committed to providing only financial data to my readers so that they can do their own analysis. I specifically do not recommend or even comment on any stocks. I am also committed to getting financial data to my readers as quickly as possible, which is why our morning newsletter comes out 30 minutes before the market opens. We also provide real-time feeds of financial data and real-time database searches to our customers as well.

After you have developed your unique selling proposition, it should become an important consideration in every future business decision you make. By making business decisions through the lens of your unique selling proposition, you are making sure that you remain committed to the key differentiating factors that set you apart from your competitors.

Action Steps:

» Talk to your potential customers about common frustrations in your industry.

» Develop your unique selling proposition.

» Consider your company's unique selling proposition when making all future business decisions.

RULE 16

Begin with a Minimum Viable Business

When you are getting started, you may be tempted to build a complete business that will scale to thousands of customers right off the bat. You may be determined to have the perfect product developed and all of the supporting systems, such as customer service software, marketing automation software and book-keeping software in place, before you do your initial launch. Resist these temptations. While it is never a bad idea to think about future goals, your initial goal is not to showcase a perfect product or grow a large business. Instead, you should be focusing on doing just enough work to validate your idea by creating a proof of concept and making sure that it is something that customers want and will pay for.

Don't Build the Perfect Product Prior to Launch

It is a natural desire to perfect your product or service before you let any customers see it. You will want to make sure all of the features you want to include are in place and that the product has been polished and fine-tuned to your liking. After all, you only get to make one first impression. However, if you wait until your product or service is absolutely perfect, you will probably never launch because you will always come up with new ideas to improve your product or service. And ultimately, building a product that is nearly perfect in your eyes is not the point. You need to switch your point of view and look at your product or service through the eyes of your customers. You do not always know how people are going to use your product or service until you actually have them

You need to look at your product or service through the eyes of your customers.

start using it. Save time and money by receiving feedback from your customers on your concept instead of building out features that they do not need or want. You may end up having to redo major portions of your product after you have received feedback from your customers. You may even realize you have built something that does not solve a problem for your customers and have to start over.

When I first started offering Analyst Ratings Network's free daily newsletter, I compiled it by hand for the first several weeks. It was only after people started subscribing, reading the newsletter, and providing feedback that I took the time to have it sent out in an automated fashion. If I had done the work to automate the newsletter delivery right away, I would have had to redo significant portions of the source code to change the newsletter to the format that best fit the subscriber's needs. By validating the idea first, I was able to make sure that I was building something that people actually wanted before spending a bunch of time and money on software development.

Solve Problems Only When They Are Actually Problems

Another temptation as you get ready to launch is to set up large and expensive solutions to take care of problems that are not actually problems yet. You should only solve problems in your business when they become problems. When you spend too much effort early on in your business focusing on far-off problems, you are wasting time and money that could be spent on things that have a more immediate impact on your business.

For example, you might go out and get a dedicated server at the cost of $250 per month with a web-hosting company so your Internet business has the capability to scale to tens of thousands of users per day. However, you can probably get away with a shared hosting account for $10.00 per month with a company like DreamHost (www.dreamhost.com) or Web Hosting Buzz (www.webhostingbuzz.com) for the first couple of years. You can make the switch to a dedicated server after your web traffic outgrows your shared hosting account and you will have eliminated a large monthly expense early on in your business. Another example would be setting up a customer service system like ZenDesk (www.zendesk.com) right away.

Just use your personal email address until it is no longer manageable. When support actually becomes a problem, then you can put your money and efforts into hiring a customer service person and setting up a customer support system.

Action Steps:

» Decide what the minimum software and services are that you will need to take your product or service and sell it to your customers.
» Create a proof of concept product to validate the idea before building out the full product or service.
» Solve problems only when they become problems.

RULE 17

Don't Give Up Equity (Early On)

In the initial stages of your Internet business, you may have limited financial resources to pay for the professional services that you will need to build your business. First, do what you can for your business by yourself. Then, depending on your skill set, you may need to hire a freelance graphic designer to create your branding or a website developer to create your website. You may need a software developer to help build the software system that powers your business or a freelance writer to help write the copy for your website. If you do not have any meaningful start-up capital, it is hard to hire people to do the work that you need to have done to grow your business. Some cash-strapped entrepreneurs will pay for professional services with equity in their business in lieu of paying cash for the services that they need, since equity is the only asset that they have. This could create issues later on as their business gains some traction, and is not as cheap as entrepreneurs believe it is in the long run.

Paying with Equity is Expensive

Paying with equity is the most expensive way to pay for graphic design, website development or content creation services if your business is successful. Just imagine that you give one website developer 10% equity in your business in exchange for designing your logo and building your e-commerce website. Five years later, you have a business that generates $1 million in revenue and $600,000 in profit each year. The website developer is long gone and you are not even using the website that they built for you when you were first getting started. Should that person get $60,000 of your profit every year because they built you a website five years ago? That is exactly what you are signing up for when you give away equity in exchange for project work like freelance writing or website development.

Good Freelancers Don't Want Equity

Most high-quality freelancers will not entertain the idea of accepting equity in lieu of cash unless the offer is from someone they already know and trust. They know that entrepreneurs who are willing to give up equity easily do not place much value in the equity of their business. They also know that equity, given away eagerly from a particular business, will likely not be worth much. Usually when a freelancer is offered equity in exchange for their services, it is from an "idea guy" who wants them to do all of the work to build his business in exchange for a small equity stake. When you try to pay for professional services with equity, you are going to have a very difficult time getting any high-quality, experienced freelancers to work with you. You will end up working with second-rate freelancers, because high-quality freelancers can easily fill up their schedule with clients who are willing to pay cash.

Consider Free and Cheaper Alternatives

You can still get your business off the ground, even if you do not have much startup capital. You can get graphic design, website development, content creation, or custom software development done. You just have to be aware of the various free and cheaper alternatives to paying a freelance writer or designer's full hourly rate. Instead of paying for a logo and a custom website design, go without a logo for a while and use a pre-built theme from a site like ThemeForest (www.themeforest.net). Use WordPress (www.wordpress.org) instead of having a custom website developed. As an alternative to paying a freelancer to write content for your site from the beginning, write it yourself and have a former teacher, friend, or family member check the grammar. If you need software development done, consider outsourcing with a more affordable developer from the Philippines in lieu of paying a U.S. firm. However, if there is a professional service that you absolutely need done but do not have the money for, it is better to go out and get a part-time job to pay for that service than to give up equity in your business.

When to Give Up Equity

Is there ever a time when you should give up equity in your business? Well, that depends on the type of business you want to build. If you want to build a large company with an office building and a few hundred employees, you will probably need to raise venture capital and give up equity to pay for that growth. If you want to build a profitable Internet business with a small remote team instead, you do not need to give up equity. If you build a business that grows organically and is profitable from the start, you can pay for growth-related expenses with the profit your company generates. I put $100 of my personal money in my business checking account when I incorporated in 2008, and every expense since then has been paid with the profit my company generates. My company currently has two employees and another five contractors who regularly do work for my company, but I own 100% of the equity in my business. My business generates more than enough revenue to pay my team members and provide for my family. I do not have to be in an office all day or share my company's profits with a venture capital firm.

Even offering equity as compensation within your business is not an ideal situation. If you have a team member who has been with you for a while and you want them to participate more in the success of your business, consider offering a profit sharing plan or give them a large bonus at the end of each year instead of giving them equity.

Action Steps:

- Hold on to the equity in your business with a tight fist. Do not give it up in exchange for professional services.
- Initially, use free and cheaper alternatives in lieu of paying a high-quality freelance rate.
- Use profit sharing plans and bonuses to reward valuable team members instead of giving up equity.

RULE 18

You Don't Need the Perfect Domain Name

As you develop a name for your business, it may be frustrating to find a good domain name that has not been used. Since the dot-com boom of the early 2000's, Internet entrepreneurs have placed an inordinate emphasis on having the perfect domain name. Some have paid large sums of money in order to acquire the perfect domain name for their Internet business. There have been at least 20 recorded instances of dot-com domain names that have sold for $1 million or more. At the top of the list is VacationRentals.com that sold for $35 million in 2007. While seven-figure domain name sales are fairly uncommon, there are thousands of five-figure and six-figure domain name sales that happen each year.

The Right Dot-Com Domain Doesn't Matter Anymore

Entrepreneurs have been willing to pay large amounts of money in order to acquire hot dot-com domain names because of their limited availability. Only one company can have the dot-com for a generic keyword, like Cars.com, Diapers.com, or Sports.com. Entrepreneurs have historically wanted these high-value, single-keyword, domain names because they are memorable and dot-com is the most commonly used top-level domain, or TLD, that companies use and customers search.

It is important to recognize that the landscape of digital real-estate is changing.

It is important to recognize that the landscape of digital real-estate is expanding. There are now 490 approved top-level domain names and the Internet Corporation for Assigned Names and Numbers, or

ICANN, is currently reviewing applications for an additional 1,800 new top-level domain names. As large companies begin to adopt their own TLDs, consumers will quickly adapt to the reality that a domain name can be anything-dot-anything instead of just anything-dot-com. Many startup companies are already using .co, .ly, .tv, and .io domain names to avoid the high cost of dot-com domain names.

As more TLDs get approved, new companies will increasingly make use of upcoming TLDs to avoid the high-cost of purchasing a dot-com domain name from a private owner. Some upcoming TLDs that have already been approved by ICANN include: .technology, .bar, .land, .solutions, .blue, .academy, .company, .today, .tips, .trade, .gift, .social, .buzz, .club, .photos, .farm, .house, .pics, .zone, .ink, .pub, .report, .foundation, and .best. Eventually there will be a critical mass of people, organizations, and companies that will opt for TLDs other than dot-com and it will be common place for domain names to end in any number of TLDs.

Single-keyword, dot-com domain names have historically had some added marketing value over other domain names because some web users will type in a keyword followed by .com into their web-browser hoping to land on the site they are looking for. The benefit of type-in traffic has been diminished in the last few years as modern web-browsers have integrated search tools directly into the address bar. Google had also once favored exact-match domain names in search results, but that ranking factor has largely been eliminated from Google's search ranking algorithm. While there were some good reasons in the past to target a single-keyword, dot-com domain name, these benefits are quickly evaporating.

How to Identify a Great Domain Name

Having the perfect dot-com domain name will probably be out of reach to you as a first-time entrepreneur because of the expense. Even if you have some capital to buy a good domain name, that money could be better used to develop your product and market your company.

If you can find a domain name that you want to use for your brand and can buy it for less than $500, it is okay to spend the money and get the domain name, but having the perfect domain name will not do anything spectacular for your business.

Here are some tips that will help you identify a great domain name for your business:

- Consider your brand name as your domain. We use GoGoPhotoContest.com instead of a generic domain like PhotoContest.com.
- Choose a domain name that can be spelled easily and can be communicated over the phone without confusion.
- Do not use a hyphenated domain name. Your customers will likely forget to type in the hyphen when going to your website.
- Use a thesaurus to identify words that are related to your industry that you could use in your domain.
- Use domain name idea generation tools like hipsterdomainfinder.com, nameboy.com, dotomator.com, and namestation.com.
- Consider using an alternative TLD instead of .com
- Consider prefixing your domain with a verb like, "get." DropBox started with the domain name, "GetDropBox.com."

RULE 19

Use Value-Based Pricing

How will you decide your price points when charging customers for your product or service? Choosing your pricing requires looking at several initial numbers and then deciding what to charge based on the value of your product or service. This is not just a matter of what you think customers might realistically pay for your product, because you may underestimate the value that you are bringing to your customers. Likewise, selecting a price based only on how much it costs you to acquire a customer or how much some similar products cost is not the right approach either. You need to determine how much value your product or service is bringing to your customers and charge them a percentage of that value. For instance, if you were to create a software-as-a-service product that saves a particular company 50 hours of work each month, you could be saving them $2,000 per month in labor costs. At most companies, it would be an easy sell to convince them to purchase a piece of software that costs $200 per month that saves them $2,000 per month in expenses.

Determine your minimum pricing based on how much it is going to cost you to acquire a customer and deliver your product or service to them. If it is going to cost you $50.00 to get a new customer through Google AdWords and another $25.00 to create and deliver your product to your customer, you cannot charge any less than $75.00 for your product without losing money. You should seek a healthy profit margin on your product or service, so consider charging around $150.00 if it costs $75.00 to win a customer and deliver the product or service to them. While you should never select a price based only on the cost of goods sold and cost of customer acquisition, knowing these numbers will help you identify the absolute minimum you can charge without losing money.

The nice thing about building products and services that are entirely digital is that there are generally few expenses that go along with them, so the total cost of customer acquisition and delivery of your product or service should be a small percentage of your company's overall revenue. In 2013, my company had a net margin of 79.8%. That means if I had only charged based on what it costs to deliver my company's products and services, I would have been leaving as much as 80% of the revenue my company made on the table. Always charge your customers based on the value that they receive and not what it costs to run your company.

Test Pricing During Your Launch

When you are first determining pricing, it will be a well-aimed shot in the dark. You know you will be providing your customers a certain amount of economic value and will charge them a percentage of that value as your fee, but there is no way to determine the price that will generate the most revenue for your company without testing your pricing. When you are launching your product, you can segment your launch list into three separate groups that receive three different price sets. If you are planning on setting a $99 price point for your product, advertise your product to one group at $79, another group at $99.00 and a third group at $129. If all three groups purchase your product at the same rate, you can safely charge the higher price to your customers. If you found that the conversion rate of the $129 group is half of the $99 group, you would certainly want to stick with the $99 price point as your final price.

There is never one perfect price for your product. Different people will be willing to pay different amounts for what you are selling, but you can get a pretty good idea of which price will generate the most revenue for your company through split-testing your pricing.

One Time Vs. Recurring Payments

There are other questions about your pricing that you need to determine besides the dollar amount you are going to charge. Are you going to sell your product or service for a one-time fee, or are you going to charge customers on a monthly or annual basis? If your product is something that your customer downloads once and does not require ongoing support, you will likely charge them a one-time fee. If you are selling them something that requires ongoing support and maintenance, like a software-as-a-service product or a membership site, you will want to charge your customers a monthly or annual rate.

Avoid offering lifetime memberships for products or services that require you to produce content or provide support on an ongoing basis. Ten years from now, you will be miserable because you will have a bunch of customers who purchased your product a decade ago who still expect you to support them. If your product or service requires you to do ongoing work, you should be charging your customers on a recurring basis.

I highly recommend building a product or service where customers pay you on a regular basis. When you build a product that people buy once, you continually have to find new customers in order to generate revenue. When you have customers who pay automatically every month, you can wake up in the morning having already made sales before ever logging on to your computer. When you have recurring revenue, you can actually take a vacation without your business grinding to a halt.

With my press release distribution business, Lightning Releases, we charge a flat fee for each press release that gets distributed. Whenever any of our past customers wants to submit another press release, we get paid again. With my investment newsletter business, customers are automatically billed $14.97 every month for the service as long as they are a customer. By offering products and services that customers pay for on a per-use or monthly basis, you will be building a steady stream of cash flow for your company.

Payment Processing Considerations

You also need to decide which payment methods you are going to accept. Many entrepreneurs make the mistake of only accepting PayPal. With my businesses, I offer both PayPal and credit card payments through Stripe (www.stripe.com). Four out of five customers choose typing in their credit card numbers over PayPal. Since you are running an Internet business, I do not recommend accepting checks or money orders. They tend to be much more of a hassle than they are worth and most customers who could pay by check will pay with another method if they are not given an option.

Create Your Refund Policy

Finally, you need to determine what your refund policy is going to be. By offering a return or refund policy, you reduce the perceived risk of your product. Your customers know that if your product or service does not work out for them, they can get a full refund on their order. I offer a 30-day money back guarantee on my company's products. Some companies offer a 60-day refund period, which is generally the maximum length a payment processor will allow you to process a refund. In my testing, I have not found a measurable difference in conversion rates when testing between a 30-day and a 60-day guarantee.

One final note on refunds: you should clearly list your refund policy on your ordering page. Every now and then you will have customers who will ask for a refund months after they purchased your product, so you will need to be able to point out where your policy is listed and politely tell them that they are not eligible for a refund.

Action Steps:

» Determine how much value your product or service will bring to your customers.
» Identify three different price points to test.
» Select which payment methods you are willing to accept.
» Write out your refund policy or guarantee.

RULE 20

Make Your Launch a Can't-Miss Event

When I launched Analyst Ratings Network's first paid product, I made the mistake of not making a big deal about the launch. The product was a premium version of the free investment newsletter that we sent out on a daily basis that included some additional benefits for those who wanted to pay for them. I had asked for some customer feedback to get ideas about what to include in the premium product, but I did not do a great job of generating buzz and excitement for the launch. When the product was ready, I simply sent out an email saying that the premium version of the newsletter was available to those who wanted it and did not do much else to promote it. At the time, there were about 10,000 people who subscribed to the free email newsletter and I only sold 30 subscriptions to the premium product. Obviously, it was not a big success.

Make a Big Deal about Your Launch

I have had subsequent launches for other products, and I have learned that you need to make a really big deal about your launch and give people incentives to sign up during your launch period. You also need to make extensive use of email marketing so that you can have a direct line of communication with your potential customers before and during your launch. When you are first starting to build a paid product, set up a can't-miss, sign-up form on your website so that people can get updates about the product as it comes along. As you are building your product, get people in your target market on your mailing list. If you already have a mailing list, you are ahead of the game. As you develop your product, you should provide periodic updates, about once or twice per month, with helpful information and the latest news about your product so the people on your list remember who you are and why they signed up for your mailing list.

Prepare Your Audience for Your Launch

When you are about a month away from your launch, you should start to send pre-launch emails that will get potential customers excited about your upcoming product. In these emails, you should remind your future users what the features and benefits of your product are, how much the product will cost, and when the product will launch. You might also include a screencast tour of your product so that users will have a better idea of how your new product or service will work. I recommend sending one email a week with the last email for your launch a few days before your product comes out. Each new email should contain some piece of information that has not been revealed in previous emails, such as any bonuses that new customers will get if they sign up during the launch period.

Creating a Launch Period

When it comes time to launch your product, think of your launch as more of a launch period rather than a launch day. This can be anywhere from two weeks to a month. Give special incentives to people who buy your product during your launch period. One way to do this is to create some sort of bonus that users will receive if they purchase during the launch period. These often come in the form of an ebook, a resource guide, a video training series or additional features with your product. During last year's Black Friday sale, we offered a 40-page investment guide called the *Trader's Guide to Equities Research*, that previously sold for $39, as a free bonus to anyone who had registered for our premium investment newsletter during the promotion.

> *Think of your launch as a launch period rather than a launch day.*

You do not need to spend a substantial amount of time creating a bonus. You may already have an older product that you can give away for free with your new product or you may know someone who will provide a product to include in your package in exchange for the contact information of the customers who purchased your product.

Use Bonuses and Time-limited Discounts

Another way to offer incentives for your users to register during your launch is to offer a time-limited discount. For example, you could give your users a 20% discount if they sign-up within the first 30 days that product is available. If your product does not have a lot of margin built into the price, raise the base price of your product by 20% and then offer a 20% discount. You will get the pricing you planned for and users will still feel like they are getting a discount. This is exactly what major department stores do by starting with high sticker prices and offering supposedly deep discounts on their products. You have to be careful with offering too many discounts though, because you may inadvertently be training your customers to only purchase when there is a discount.

A Sample Launch Schedule

During your launch period, you should send out a series of emails extolling the features and benefits of your product. Here is a sample schedule for emails to send out with a product that has a 21-day launch window:

28 Days before Launch: announce the launch date and remind your users about the features and benefits of your product.

21 Days before Launch: answer a list of frequently asked questions about your product.

14 Days before Launch: upload a video tour or screencast of the product.

7 Days before Launch: announce the bonuses that users will receive if they register during the launch period.

1 Day before Launch: send a reminder of the launch date/time, bonuses, and pricing.

Launch Day: announce that the product is available and provide a link to sign-up for the product.

4 Days after Launch: send another email that contains the frequently asked questions about your product.

8 Days after Launch: send your subscribers some social proof, often in the form of testimonials, about the rave reviews your product has received.

12 Days after Launch: remind your users of what pain your product solves and the features and benefits of your product.

16 Days after Launch: remind your users about the bonuses and discount that they will receive if they sign-up during the launch period

20 Days after Launch: announce that tomorrow is the last day to receive the discount and bonus.

21 Days after Launch: announce that the launch period is ending today and that it is the last day to get the discount and bonus.

Have a Clear End to Your Launch Period

It is also important to have a defined end date for your launch period. While many of your users will make purchases on the first few days that your product is available, you will find that other potential customers are procrastinators and will wait until the last possible moment to purchase your product. By having a defined end-date of your launch period, you create a sense of urgency to encourage your customers to sign-up before the discount and bonuses are discontinued. Typically about 25% of the people who register for a product during a launch period will do so in the last couple days of the launch if you have a clearly defined end-date for your launch period and send the appropriate emails to your list telling them that the launch is coming to an end.

Action Steps:

- » Create a landing page to collect email addresses for your launch.
- » Grow your email list with blogs, videos, and conversations on social media with your potential customers.
- » Develop a calendar of emails you are going to send before and during your launch period.
- » Set a clear end-date for your product's discounts and bonuses.

Running Your Business

RULE 21

Get Your Finances Right from the Beginning

When you are first starting your business, you may have signed up to become a corporation or an LLC without fully understanding the ramifications of that decision. You may be mixing your personal income and expenses with your business's income and expenses. You may only have a random collection of receipts in a shoe-box to hand to your tax person at the end of the year, assuming you bothered to file your taxes at all. This is not a winning game plan. You will not have a good idea of how much money your company is making or not making and you will end up with a major mess to clean up when you have to file your taxes.

How to Screw Up Your Company's Finances

When I first started my company, American Consumer News, LLC, in 2008, I was participating in a small accelerator program offered by Dakota State University. It was the first year they offered the program and they arranged for a lawyer to set up my LLC and take care of any other necessary paperwork to start my business from a legal perspective. The attorney had me file IRS Form 8832, which would make my company taxable as an S-Corporation. I signed that form along with a lot of other paperwork that I did not understand. Being an S-Corporation has some nice tax benefits, but I was wholly unaware that I needed to be doing payroll and paying myself a salary, complete with the paperwork and everything else that comes along with it. I was not paying payroll tax or Federal and state unemployment taxes on the part of my income that would have been labeled my salary.

Three years later, I asked a local accountant about setting up an individual 401(K) plan, and in reply he asked me a question along the lines of, "You are paying yourself a salary, right?" Of course, I was not. He went on to explain that I needed to re-file the last three years' worth of tax returns and would have to pay payroll taxes on all of the income that I had earned during that time. I kicked myself for the next couple of weeks for not bothering to take the time to understand what I was signing up for when I set up my business.

Fortunately, I jumped through all of the appropriate hoops and got everything set straight. I had to register myself as an employee with the State of South Dakota, set up state and federal unemployment taxes, and re-file three years' worth of corporate and personal tax returns. I ended up writing checks for several thousand dollars to the IRS to take care of the issue.

I found out that I had also neglected to register for a sales tax license with the Department of Revenue. Thankfully, the vast majority of my company's revenue is through advertising and most of my customers are out of state, so my tax bill was small. The South Dakota Department of Revenue was pretty nice about the situation and helped me become compliant with state law. If you are not sure when you are supposed to collect sales tax or when you are supposed to pay Use tax, see if your state puts on workshops periodically; most do. That workshop will teach you the ins-and-outs of sales and Use tax.

Best Practices

I could have avoided these headaches if I had done a few basic things right from the start. First, fully understand the legal structure under which your company is operating. There are different tax forms that you need to file depending on whether or not you are operating as a sole proprietor, a limited liability company, or a corporation. If you have not filed any paperwork, you will be operating as a sole proprietor by default, which is just fine until your company starts to make significant amounts of money. I recommend waiting until you are making around $100,000 a year before you switch to a corporate structure. It is definitely worthwhile to pay an accountant in your area when you are first getting started so you know exactly what taxes you should be paying and when you should be paying them.

Second, you need to think of your business as a separate person from yourself for financial purposes. You should have a separate checking account for your business. You should pay all of your business expenses out of this account and deposit all of your business earnings into this account. At the end of the month, or at the end of the quarter if that works better for you, your business should write you a check for the profit your company made. That way, you will have a simple listing of your company's income and expenses whenever you receive your bank statement and know exactly how much profit you made. If you use this strategy, your accountant should not have a mess to deal with at the end of the year.

Dealing with Taxes

As a general rule, take a quarter of whatever you take home as profit and put it in a separate savings account for taxes. When you are an employee of a company, taxes are automatically taken out of your paycheck and you never really miss the money that gets sent to the IRS. Unfortunately, small business owners often forget about setting money aside to pay their taxes and end up with a big tax bill at the end of the year. By setting aside money in a separate account specifically for your quarterly tax estimates, you can avoid the temptation to spend the money that you owe to the IRS on other things. More information about quarterly estimates can be found on the IRS website. (*http://www.irs.gov/uac/Form-1040-ES,-Estimated-Tax-for-Individuals-1*).

Remember that the IRS should always be paid first. They are the only entity that can send you to prison for not paying your bills. If you run into trouble, you cannot bankrupt out of any debt that you owe the IRS and if you get behind, the penalties and interest can be enormous. Whether you are just paying quarterly estimates or have employees and are doing quarterly returns on your company's payroll, paying the IRS is not optional.

Online Tracking Tools

Finally, if your Internet business makes use of payment processing services like PayPal, Square, or Stripe, consider using online bookkeeping software like Xero (www.xero.com), Quickbooks Online (quickbooksonline.com), or Outright (www.outright.com). These services will automatically import transactions from your bank, PayPal and other payment processors. They will tell you exactly what your company earned during a specific period of time and provide a number of helpful charts and graphs which will help identify trends in your business. Your accountant will also be much happier with you for having good financial records from what these services create automatically.

Action Steps:

» Learn what taxes you should be paying and when you should be paying them.

» Open a separate checking account for your business and a separate savings account for your quarterly estimates.

» Use an online bookkeeping system like Quickbooks Online or Xero.

» Keep your online bookkeeping system up-to-date to identify trends and avoid end-of-the-year headaches.

RULE 22

Busyness Is Not Productivity

A few years back, I became friends with another entrepreneur whom I will call Mark. He did a great job of building vertical news websites similar to some of the sites that I have built like American Banking and Market News. If you did not look too closely, you would think that the websites he built and the websites I built were produced by the same company. Although we had very similar businesses at the time, he was never able to gain the traction that my company had. For a while I could not figure out what the difference was between our two companies, until I saw how Mark used his time. Whenever I chatted with him on Skype and asked him what he was working on, he would tell me that he was doing things like working on a logo, trying out different plug-ins on his websites, moderating comments or working on the formatting of his articles. Mark did everything himself and spent a lot of time working on his business, but his time was not well spent at all. Instead of focusing on the core components of his business, where his income is generated, he regularly got distracted by ancillary tasks that did not directly tie into generating revenue. He never put together a team or created systems to help run his business more efficiently. While he was spending a lot of time working, he was never that productive because he was too busy working on the wrong things.

Productivity and busyness are not the same. In this context, busyness is spending time working on your company without regard to what you are actually accomplishing. Productivity is completing specific tasks that bring you closer to accomplishing your business goals. You must use your time wisely, leverage software, and create a team to be truly productive in your business. There are some weeks where I may do as few as 20 hours of actual work, but I am still using those hours to effectively move my business forward. I rely heavily on software automation and my team members to conduct the day-to-day operations of my business. I work on identifying specific tasks that will move my business forward and have my team members execute those tasks. I also use software tools to automate regular and repetitive tasks. For example, I use ManageWP to automatically update WordPress and related plug-ins on my websites instead of manually running updates on each site. Instead of keeping track of individual revenue and expense items, I use software to automatically compile and categorize transactions from Stripe, PayPal, and my bank into a bookkeeping system so I always know how much money my company is or is not making without having to manually put reports together.

Focus on Key Revenue Generating Tasks

In order to stay focused on the activities that matter the most in your business, take the time to identify the specific tasks in your business that are directly tied to generating revenue and spend the majority of your time on those tasks. In other words, what needs to happen in order for your company to make money? These tasks are closely tied to revenue generation and will vary depending on what type of Internet business you start, but they will certainly include key marketing and sales activities as well as product delivery and support.

Identify the specific tasks in your business that are directly tied to generating revenue.

If you knew that the vast majority of your new customers would come from referrals from your existing customers, you would make sure you spent a lot of time working on collecting referrals, even if it meant some other less important things did not get done. For GoGo Photo Contest, we know that the activities closely tied to revenue generation are those that bring awareness about our product to animal shelters, those that help shelters that have expressed interest in our contest set up their own contests, and those that educate the shelters we partner with to show them how to promote their contest well. There are many other things we could spend our time doing, but as long as we do those three things well, we will make money. It is okay to let your business get a little rough around the edges. Your company will not fall apart if you forget to moderate the comments on your blog or if you do not get around to tweaking your web site's design. Do not do peripheral tasks well at the expense of doing your key revenue generating poorly.

Eliminate Distractions When Working

When you are working on completing a specific task, stay focused. You will be able to get twice as much work done if you focus on completing a single task at a time and remove all potential distractions. You can get rid of distractions by putting your phone on silent, turning off email notifications and closing programs that are likely to interrupt your work, such as Skype. You may also consider using a program that will prevent you from accessing social media sites for a set period of time, like Anti-Social (www.anti-social.cc) or LeechBlock (addons.mozilla.org/en-US/firefox/addon/leechblock/), so that you will not be tempted to take a quick break to check Facebook or Twitter. If you want to measure your productivity and set goals for avoiding distractions, consider using a service like RescueTime (www.rescuetime.com) which will monitor your computer use and tell you what programs and websites you spend the most time on. RescueTime will tell you the hard truth about how much of your computer time you actually use for work and how much time you spend playing games or browsing Facebook and Twitter.

Improve Productivity with the Pomodoro Technique

Consider using the Pomodoro Technique if you are having a hard time staying focused or motivating yourself to work on your business. The Pomodoro Technique is a simple system that will enable you to do short bursts of work while mitigating distractions and preventing burn-out. To use the Pomodoro Technique, identify one thing that you want to get done. Set a timer for 25 minutes and work on nothing but that task until the timer rings. When the timer rings, take a five minute break to clear your mind and repeat the process over again. After you have gone through four Pomodoro sessions, take a longer break so that your brain can recharge. This system will help you stay focused because you know that you have a break coming up at the end of the 25 minutes and you are scheduling time to clear your mind in between sprints of working. To learn more about the Pomodoro Technique, visit www.pomodorotechnique.com.

Action Steps:

- Identify the key tasks that cause your company to generate income.
- Silence your smartphone and turn off all notifications when working.
- Consider using RescueTime to track your productivity.
- Try out the Pomodoro Technique.

RULE 23

Don't Be an Employee in Your Business

If you are planning on starting a new business, take care not to spend too much time working as an employee in your business and not enough time as the business owner working on your business. This is the core message of the book, *E-Myth*, by Michael Gerber. As a new entrepreneur, you probably have a strong technical background in providing the specific service or product your company sells from your past work experiences, but you may lack experience in managing a business, which is what you need as an owner who runs the company that sells your product or service.

For example, if you were to open an auto service shop, chances are you would already be an experienced mechanic. But spending your time fixing cars to generate revenue for your business is not the best use of your time as an owner. While doing the repair work is an important component of auto service, you have other work to do. You must learn to delegate work to other employees whom you have chosen because of their experience. Then, you need to spend as much of your time as possible on tasks that only you as the owner can do: identifying your company's mission, vision and values; creating and managing teams; developing a marketing and sales plan; learning about industry trends; reviewing the company's key performance indicators and following-through with strategic planning.

When to Outsource and Delegate

While it is easy to think that some of the tasks of working on and growing your business are a luxury for companies with dozens of employees, the principal still applies if you are a one or two person company. Even if you are a one person company, you should not be doing everything in your business. There are real benefits to leveraging the talent and abilities of others. Even when you are just getting started, only perform the tasks that you have real expertise in and try to afford to hire someone relatively cheaply to perform the other parts of the process where you lack proficiency. For example, you probably should not be doing your own book-keeping and accounting. For a relatively small amount of money, you can hire an accountant to do your taxes and keep track of your books. If you are not a graphic designer, you probably should not be designing your logo. If you are not a front-end web developer, you probably should not be designing your own website. If you are not a marketing person, you probably should not be writing your own ad-copy. There are a ton of talented individuals on places like Elance (www.elance.com) and Odesk (www.Odesk.com) who you can hire to do things that you do not know how to do for a lot less money than you might think.

You should also outsource or delegate any task that you can have done for cheaper than your time is worth. If your business made $100,000 last year, your time is worth $50 per hour assuming you work a standard 2,000 hour work year. If you can pay someone $12 an hour to do customer service work for your company and you choose not to hire someone to do the work, you are effectively paying yourself $12 per hour to perform customer service work in your company. Knowing that your time is worth $50 an hour, you would never go out and take a part-time customer service job for another company that pays $12 an hour, but by not hiring that job out to a contractor or an employee, you are effectively working for yourself at $12 an hour. If you are working on a $12 an hour task which prevents you from working on a $50 an hour task, you are actually losing $38 an hour by not paying someone else to work for you.

Bringing On Team Members

Hiring contractors from marketplaces like Elance and Odesk are a great way to tackle one-time tasks. For tasks that need to be repeated on a regular basis, like data entry, social media marketing, and customer service, you should probably find someone to bring to your team as an employee or a virtual assistant. Hiring a virtual assistant using a service like Virtual Staff Finder (www.

virtualstafffinder.com) can be great for some less complex tasks, but for the critical operations of your business, I still prefer to hire someone locally as an employee so you are working with someone you know, like, and trust. An employee does not necessarily need to work in the same place as you do, but it should be someone who is competent and who will probably be around for a while.

When is the right time to bring on another team member? I think a good rule of thumb is when you have enough work to fill up at least half of their time. Last Spring, I created a half-time position with my company to do customer support, data entry, and a few other administrative tasks. When I hired my employee, I probably only had about ten-hour's worth of work for her to do a week. I knew my company was growing, so it was not hard to find additional tasks to fill up her time, and after a few months had passed I saw that she was capable of doing a range of work for my company.

You might think hiring your first employee is a big, scary proposition, but it is not. You will know whether or not your company generates enough revenue to pay your employee's salary based on what your company has made for the last few months. Your accountant can easily setup things like payroll services and state and federal unemployment. You can use a discount broker like Vanguard (www.vanguard.com) to setup a retirement plan for your company. If you want to help your employee out with health insurance, likely your best bet is to give them a set amount of money and have them buy their own policy on one of the new state exchanges. There is certainly some administrative work when hiring a new employee, but it is not an impossible task.

Standard Operating Procedures

When you are preparing to hire an employee or bring on a contractor, I recommend creating a series of Standard Operating Procedures (SOP) for the various tasks that they will be performing. Each SOP should contain a description of the task, an explanation of why the task is important, and what role it plays in your business. There should be a series of specific steps that the employee should perform when completing the task and an explanation of why it is important to perform that task using the method you outlined. That way, your employee will have good documentation about the jobs that they need to perform for your business when they first get started and you will know that your employee is completing tasks exactly the way that you want them to complete it. A month before my employee started working for my company, I outlined the specific tasks that she would be doing and created an SOP for each task for her to refer to. I also created a document that contains the most common issues and questions our customers have and how to take care of them, so she knew how to answer the vast majority of questions that our customers are going to ask immediately after purchasing a product or service. If my employee were to ever move on to a different job with another company, I would still have the SOP and documentation available to streamline the training process for any future employee who has to do the tasks she is doing right now.

There are some tasks that you do not need an employee to tackle these days. There are great tools available which allow you to automate certain repetitive tasks, including Zapier (www.zapier.com), which is a paid product, and the service, If This Then That (www.ifttt.com) which is free.

With Zapier and If This Then That, you can automatically:

- » Post new blog posts to Facebook, Twitter, and LinkedIn.
- » Add new email contacts to a MailChimp email list or a Google Spreadsheet.
- » Sync files between DropBox, SkyDrive, and Google Drive.
- » Save Tweets, Facebook posts, and Emails to a Google Spreadsheet.
- » Add events to your calendar from an RSS feed or other public calendar.
- » Log your phone calls and SMS messages in a spreadsheet.
- » Receive weather alerts via your smartphone or email.
- » Thank new followers on Twitter for following you.
- » Save Gmail attachments in DropBox.
- » Mute or un-mute your phone based on your location or the time of day.
- » Invite new email contacts to connect on LinkedIn.

To get other ideas for possible uses for these tools, visit the Zapier Explore page at zapier.com/app/explore and the IFTTT recipes page at ifttt.com/recipes. If you are a software developer or know a software developer who does good work, you can begin to automate major portions of your online business. For example, the daily investment newsletter that my company publishes is sent out automatically each morning without any intervention from any staff member of my company. The data that makes up the newsletter is automatically gathered from a variety of sources every morning, which then gets compiled by software into the actual newsletter, which then gets automatically sent out to anyone who has an active subscription using SendGrid's SMTP mailing service.

You are certainly going to have to do a lot of work in your business when you first get started, but as you grow, you can begin to outsource, delegate, and automate the majority of the tasks that are required to make your business happen so that you are free to work on your business rather than in your business.

Action Steps:

- » Identify what tasks you are currently performing in your business that you should be paying someone else to do.
- » Create Standard Operating Procedures (SOP) for tasks that you need to delegate or outsource.
- » Automate repetitive tasks using IFTTT or Zapier.

RULE 24

Befriend Your Customers

Some entrepreneurs see their customers as just another part of their business system, like marketing and accounting. They think of their customers as a homogeneous group and fail to recognize that they are in business because hundreds or thousands of individual people have decided to buy their products or services. This is especially tempting if you have a low-price-point business or have an automated sales process. When you see customers as numbers on a screen, it can be easy to forget that they are real people. Avoid this mistake. The relationships that you have with individual customers will be the best way to get feedback about what your company is doing right, what it is doing wrong, and what it should do next.

Maintaining Customer Relationships

You should actively work to maintain the relationships that you have with your customers. If you have a higher-price-point business and only have a handful of customers, touch base with them on a periodic basis to remain personable and see if you can help them. Build rapport with them and take an interest in their personal lives. You might consider sending birthday cards or small gifts during holidays. If you have a lower-price-point business and have hundreds or thousands of customers, you will have to use different strategies to help maintain your relationships with customers. After a customer buys your product, consider setting up an auto-responder series where your customers will get an email with tips or advice every ten days for the first six months after they buy your product. That will provide them additional value and help keep your company fresh in their minds.

Do Customer Service Well

Because you are building an Internet business, there will be customers who buy your product or service through your website and never respond again. There is not much you can or even necessarily need to do about that, because there will be plenty of customers who will email you with feedback or ask for help. When dealing with customer service issues, be as helpful as possible and respond to requests quickly. Do not reply with an automated message that tells them you will respond within a few business days. Automated messages make your customers think you have responded to them, but leave them disappointed when their question is not actually answered in the email. Instead, just do customer service where you can respond to customer service emails within a day like you would with any other email. Make sure to respond personally with your name in the signature so that your customers can make a connection with a real person to the email you send. Be flexible about refund and payment policies. It is usually better to refund a customer's money than to have them be mad at your company and gripe about it to others. I recommend that you do your own customer service for at least the first six months of running your business so that you know exactly what issues your customers are facing when your product or service is first getting off the ground.

Get Feedback Early and Often

Ask for feedback from your customers early and often. Ask them what they like and do not like about your company's products and services. Ask them what they would change about your company's offerings if they could. Ask them what kinds of products and services they wish your company offered. When you are planning on launching a new product or service, remember to ask for feedback before starting product development work. One of the best ways to make sure that you get helpful feedback on a regular basis is to automatically send your customers an email asking for feedback a week after they purchase your product. Here is the email that I send out to ARN Daily Premium Subscribers seven days after they subscribe:

> *Hi-*
>
> *I wanted to take a second to check in with you and see how your subscription to ARN Daily Premium is going and let you know about*

a couple of web-based features that are included with your ARN Daily Premium account.

First, you can access your newsletter on the Analyst Ratings Network website by clicking on this link. Just click the "ARN Daily Premium" link in the top left of the page to generate a fresh copy of your newsletter at any time of the day.

Second, check out the "Company Profiles" and "EarningsDB" pages linked from your account management page when you get a chance. The "Company Profiles" page provides a summary of recent ratings, earnings and headlines for any publicly traded company. The "EarningsDB" page allows you to search through earnings history by company, sector, industry, beat/miss % and a number of other metrics.

Finally, I'd love to get your feedback about your subscription to ARN Daily Premium so far. How are we doing? Are you getting value out of your daily email newsletter? What can we do to improve our service?

Thanks!
Matthew Paulson
Analyst Ratings Network

Action Steps:

- Take an active interest in your customers and work to maintain your relationship with them.
- Respond to customer service requests quickly and personally.
- Regularly ask for feedback from your customers about your company's products and services.

RULE 25

Not Everyone Needs to Be Your Customer

On the other hand, befriending your customers and getting to know them personally lets you experience a hard truth: there are some customers who are simply more trouble than they are worth. There are some customers who will not be satisfied regardless of how much you bend over backwards to help them. They make unrealistic demands for what they are paying. They constantly ask for changes and new features to your product. They think they deserve a discount just because they asked for one. They want a refund when your service has the slightest hiccup. They waste your time with an endless stream of questions and complaints. Well, your customers have the right to stop paying you and quit doing business with you at any time and I think it is okay for you to have the same right.

I learned this lesson while working for a former employer as a web developer. Most of our projects went relatively smoothly, but every now and then we had a customer who was off the wall. There was one customer in particular who insisted on having multiple meetings per week while he worked on his project. He would frequently make requests to move an image 1 pixel to the left or make very slight color changes to his website that no one would notice but him. We would receive multiple emails from him each day. When he asked for a custom events module for his website which was not in his proposal, I politely told him that we could do it but that it would likely cost extra. He pounded his fist on the table and yelled, "#$%& it! I paid for a custom events calendar, I WANT CUSTOM EVENTS!" During the final week before his website launched, he actually wanted to work out of our office so that he could direct us as we finished his project. We probably ended up putting twice as many hours into the project than we should have because of the client's constant change requests and unusual demands. I do not know if the company ended up making money off the deal, but I could have certainly done without having him as a client.

Now, don't get me wrong. This is not to say that you should see your customers as the enemy or a source of contempt. The vast majority of your customers will be happy to give you money for the value that you provide them. They may run into an issue every now and then and need help fixing something and you should politely and happily take care of their issues. Having great customer service is one of the best ways to keep customers around for a long time. Zappos built a multi-million dollar e-commerce business by having a legendary customer service department. You should do everything you reasonably can for your customers to make sure they are happy with your service. That being said, there are just some people who will not be happy no matter what you do and it is okay to decide to stop doing business with them.

Some people will not be happy and it is okay to stop doing business with them.

Identifying a Problem Customer

You will recognize your problem customer fairly quickly. You already know who they are based on how many times they have called or emailed you with their problems. They are more than likely on one of your lower payment tiers. They ask for things that are not included with your product or service. They regularly ask for discounts and refunds. They send you long winded emails asking for help or making requests. They may attack you personally. They often complain and do not seem to be terribly concerned with whether or not their problem actually gets fixed.

If you can identify problem customers before they become your customers, you can save yourself time and troubles later on. When you talk to a prospective customer, there are several warning signs that will help you identify whether or not they could be more trouble than they are worth. Potential problem customers may ask you to do a smaller, significantly discounted project, or even free work in exchange for a potentially bigger project down the road. If they are not willing to pay your market rate on the first project, they will not want to pay your market rate on any future projects either. More than likely, any promises of a bigger and more lucrative project down the road will not pan out. Potential problem customers will ask you an endless series of questions about your company's products and services. They may try to convince you how great a deal working with them would be, despite the fact that they are nameless online. They may try to get you to sign long-form non-disclosure agreements or other contracts before signing up for your product or service.

Dealing with Problem Customers

The best way to deal with potential problem customers is to not cater to all of their demands. You should certainly provide a reasonable effort to answer their questions as you would any potential customer, but you should not spend several hours trying to answer their questions, sign any legal papers they put in front of you, or give them a significant discount just because they asked for one, unless they bring you a massive amount of business and you decide that it is worth it. If they send you a long winded email, answer it briefly and do not waste your time on them. As soon as the potential problem customer figures out that they cannot push you around, they will probably wander off and waste someone else's time. If they do not leave on their own, it is okay to send them a polite message and say, "I'm sorry, but I don't think we're going to be a good fit for you or be able to meet your needs. You may want to check out X, Y, or Z company that may be able to offer what you're looking for."

Refund Liberally

Sometimes you will not be able to identify a problem customer until they have already paid you. With the first few issues that they have, you should give the customer the benefit of the doubt, but after awhile it will be hard to continue dealing with your problem customer. It is okay to say no to their unreasonable demands. Tell them politely that their extra or unusual requests are not part of the product or service that you offer. If they continue to complain, you can apologize and offer a refund, saying, "I'm sorry we will not be able to accommodate your request. If you would like, we can cancel your order and refund your payment." More often than not, they will take the offer of the refund and go on their way. Give yourself permission to walk away from that problem customer. You will spend much more time and money than they originally paid you trying to keep them happy. You are better off giving them their money back and sending them on their way.

Action Steps:

- » Do not bend over backwards for people who have not committed to hiring you yet.
- » Give yourself permission to let problem customers go.
- » Liberally and politely offer refunds to problem customers and be done with them.

RULE 26

Read Before You Sign

As you build your business, you will enter into contractual agreements with companies much larger than your own. These agreements often come into play for things like website hosting, consulting services, marketing deals, and managing advertising sales. Typically the larger company will have a standard contract written by their legal department that they provide to all of their partners. Many entrepreneurs make the mistake of signing these agreements without having a clear understanding of what they are agreeing to do. The contract you are presented with will likely be skewed heavily in favor of the company that wrote it, but entrepreneurs sign these agreements thinking they will never actually come into play and end up signing bad deals as a result. Also, as the smaller party in the deal, a newer entrepreneur may think that the terms of the agreements they are offered are non-negotiable. This is usually not the case.

Contract Horror Stories

There have been several occasions where I have been offered a contract with a company to do some consulting work or an advertising deal that had untenable terms. One specific company gave me an agreement that they use with a much larger vendor that also did software projects for them. They did a copy-and-paste job with the agreement. I was going to do a relatively small software project for them, and the agreement contained terms I could not agree to as a single-person vendor. For example, the contract would have required me to legally defend the other company in the event of a lawsuit. I pointed out the various problems with that agreement and fortunately they agreed to a simple one-page contract outlining the work I would be doing for them.

On another occasion, there was a large advertising company

that wanted to represent my email list to advertisers for the purpose of selling dedicated emails and newsletter sponsorships. The agreement presented to me required that they serve as the exclusive representation of my list and gave them a credit on their invoice for the value of any other commercial promotions I did with my distribution list. That meant I would not have been able to do any affiliate marketing or any list swaps to my own email list without paying them for it. This company would not budge on the terms, so I ended up talking to two of their competitors to see what they could do. I ended up with a list representation deal that had a better revenue share, higher CPMs and far less onerous contractual terms.

Take the Time to Read Legal Documents

The key to avoiding bad deals is to actually read the agreements that a company sends you. For most contracts, you probably do not need a lawyer to comb through every detail of a written agreement, but you should take the time to read through any legal paperwork that a larger company sends you and asks you to sign. If you are not sure about what some section of an agreement says, ask. If there are terms in the agreement that you cannot agree to, tell them. They may send you a revised contract that does not contain the objectionable terms. There have been several times when companies much larger than my own have changed the terms of an agreement at my request.

Be Mindful of Employment Documents

Keep track of whether or not you have signed any legal agreements with your current or former employers. Some employers require their employees to sign contracts to turn over any intellectual property the employee develops to the company while under the employment of said company. This means if you are working for a company and you find a formula that cures cancer on your own time, they own the formula. Employers often have employees sign non-compete agreements that prevent them from developing competing products or soliciting their employer's clients for a period of two or three years after they stop working at the company. Typically you will sign these types of agreements on your first day of work and forget about them, but they can come back to haunt you after you finish working for an employer. This is particularly true if you have a lot of success and your former employer takes notice. If you plan on quitting your job or have recently quit your job to pursue your business full-time, review any agreements you have signed with your current or former employers to make sure you are not pursuing anything on your own that might result in a lawsuit. The enforceability of these types of agreements can vary a lot from state to state. If you plan on violating the terms of any agreement you signed, run it past a lawyer first.

Don't Do Handshake Deals

Finally, if you decide to enter into some sort of business partnership with another small company, take the time to write out a simple contract. Do not do handshake deals. Have a one or two page agreement that outlines the rights, responsibilities, and payment terms for both parties. The agreement does not need to be large or complex, but you should have something in writing so that there is no question about the agreement between you and the other company.

Action Steps:

- » Read every contract presented to you before you sign on the dotted line.
- » Review any legal agreements you have made with your current or former employer.
- » Do not do handshake deals. Get it in writing.

RULE 27

Measure Your Company's Vital Signs

How can you tell if your business is doing well or on the brink of failure? You can guess based on your estimation of how busy you think your company is, but having customers walking through your virtual door can be deceiving. If you really want to know how your business is doing in any given week or month, take the time to understand your business's key metrics, commonly referred to as key performance indicators, or KPIs, and measure them on a periodic basis. By doing this, you effectively take the vital signs of your business by tracking its key metrics.

In real life, you go for a physical checkup and when your doctor tells you that you have high blood pressure, it means there is something wrong with your body and you need to address it to avoid more serious issues. By taking the time to get your vitals checked, you have the ability to address the issue before it leads to a heart attack. In a similar way, when you check your business's vital signs, you can identify potentially serious problems before they make a significant impact on your company's bottom line.

Identify serious problems before they make a significant impact on your bottom line.

Actionable Metrics vs. Vanity Metrics

The key is to recognize the most important metrics of your business and monitor them on a regular basis. Unfortunately, entrepreneurs tend to track the wrong numbers. These are known as vanity metrics. Some examples of vanity metrics include: your followers on Facebook and Twitter, your Klout score, the amount of traffic your website gets and the total number of email addresses or registered users you have. Vanity metrics are often lifetime totals that almost always go, "up and to the right" regardless of how well your business is doing at any one time. Vanity metrics are easily manipulated. They have a tendency to make the entrepreneur feel good about the growth of their business, but do not correlate well to the numbers that really matter. The metrics that you should be tracking will be actionable and tell the story of how your business is doing right now. Actionable metrics will provide you with specific insight into certain components of your business over a specific period of time. They should also help you decide what actions you need to take to move your business forward.

For example, the premium version of my investment newsletter, ARN Daily Premium, is available for a monthly fee to my subscribers. A few months back, the rate at which subscribers canceled increased by about 60% from one month to the next. While my monthly revenue had not taken a significant hit yet, I knew that something was wrong with the newsletter or that I may have upset some of my customers. It turns out that the newsletter wasn't tracking stock prices correctly and the newsletter's formatting was broken for AOL users. I was able to address those two issues and the cancellation dropped back down to where it had been previously. Because I was tracking that metric, I was able to identify and address the problem before it became a more serious issue.

Here are some examples of actionable metrics you should be tracking in your business:

Customer Acquisition Costs

» How much money do you need to spend to acquire a new customer?

» Is it costing you more or less than it was last month to get a new customer?

Conversion Rates

» What percent of the people who land on your website buy your product?

» Is that number increasing or decreasing?

Referral Sources

» Which sources of traffic are sending you the most new customers?

» How can you maximize the number of customers they send you?

User Growth

- How many users registered in the last month?
- Do you see an increase in new user registration from the previous month?

Active Users

- How many people are actively using your product this month?
- Are most of your customers currently using your product or services more or less than they were last month?

Lifetime Value

- How much is each customer worth to you while they are your customer?
- Is that number increasing or decreasing?

Churn Rate

- What percentage of your users are canceling or leaving each month?
- Are there sudden changes in these numbers?

Revenue and Profit

- How much did your company earn last month?
- How much profit did you make?
- Did you make more money than the previous month?

The metrics that are most important to you will be specific to your business, but the examples above show the types of metrics that you should track. When you first get started, you can track these numbers on a monthly basis using an excel spreadsheet. When your business starts to operate at scale, you can have a developer track these numbers through software or start making use of dashboard software that will track them for you.

Action Steps:

- Understand the difference between actionable metrics and vanity metrics.
- Create a list of the most important metrics you should track on a regular basis.
- Track your company's actionable metrics monthly.

RULE 28

Be Skeptical. Be Aware.

If you run your own business and have any measure of success, you are a major target for scam artists. As an entrepreneur, you are seen as someone who is more successful and who has more money than the average person. Scammers see companies as large, faceless organizations and do not think they are hurting an actual person by finding a way to steal money from your company. Other scam artists see you as a greedy, wealthy, business owner and think that this perception justifies stealing money from you. When you run your own business, it is a matter of when, not if, you are going to be targeted by one scam or another.

Common External Scams

The first time my company was targeted with fraud was in 2008, just after I incorporated. The name of my company is: American Consumer News, LLC. Another company with a similar name claimed they owned the phrase, "American Consumer," and demanded I pay $7,500 per year to license the name from them. They sent a threatening letter from an attorney in an attempt to intimidate me. I assumed their accusation was unfounded since the phrase, "American Consumer," is generic and probably could not be trademarked. I paid an attorney to respond to their letter and tell them to get lost. I did not hear from them again.

As a business owner, be prepared to receive a lot of fake invoices in the mail. There are companies that scan domain name registration information and send you fake renewal notices via snail mail. They are never the company you originally registered the domain with and often ask 10 times the going rate. If you ever file for a trademark or patent, you will get inundated with fake invoices. When I filed for a trademark for the name, "Analyst Ratings Network," I got several invoices for as much as $2,300 for supposed international trademark registration services. Pay close attention to the invoices that you receive and keep track of your domain name, trademarks, and purchases. If you did not order it, do not pay it.

Internal Scams

As your business expands to the point where it is affordable and necessary for you to hire team members to share the workload, hire people you trust. There has only been one time during my career where one of my team members tried to steal money from me. I had a writer who sent me invoices for some articles that he did not write. It took me a few months to catch on to what he was doing. I was not proactive in verifying the work he said he was doing, so his deception went on longer than it should have. I ended up losing about $1,500 from that ordeal, which shows why it is always a good idea to trust but verify. If you run an online business, take steps to make sure you do not get hit with internal fraud. Do not let your team members have access to your checks, credit cards, or online payment accounts such as Pay Pal. If you only have a handful of team members, it is easy to pay all of the bills yourself. This is a benefit that entrepreneurs with relatively small, online businesses have that larger companies do not.

Protecting Your Financial Accounts

There are particular steps that you need to take with your bank accounts as a business owner. Consumer checking accounts and credit cards have much stronger fraud protection regulations than business accounts do. I recommend getting a separate personal credit card and using it as your business credit card so that you can enjoy the same protections under the law that personal credit cards have. You will also want to be particularly careful with checks. Keep them locked in a safe or lockbox in your home or office when not in use. If you are running an online business and most of your expenses are services like web hosting and advertising, ideally you will only have to write a few checks, which will limit your exposure to check fraud.

You will also want to protect your online credentials for your financial accounts by using strong passwords and making sure that your computer does not get infected with malware. I recommend having a separate password for your email account, your financial accounts, and one for everything else you use online. If you want to get really fancy, use a password manager like Last Pass to ensure you have a unique password for every website you visit. To prevent malware from attacking your computer, use a modern web browser like Fire Fox or Google Chrome and run anti-virus software. Alternatively, buy a Mac.

Insurance for Your Internet Business

Finally, you need to make sure you have good liability policies in place for both yourself and your business. If you have any meaningful amount of money, you should look at getting a personal liability policy to provide home and auto liability above and beyond what your homeowner and car insurance policies offer. For your business, you should look into an Errors and Omissions policy that will protect your company if you make a mistake and end up costing someone money. You might want to look at a Business Interruption policy that will pay you if your business is interrupted by a server issue or other event. Talk to an independent insurance agent to make sure you are getting the right coverage for your specific type of business once you hit a reasonable revenue level.

These steps and suggestions will help you take healthy, preventative measures against the possibility of scams. As an entrepreneur, you should not spend extra time worried about how someone is going to defraud your company. But, being aware that it does occur and making smart decisions to limit fraud from affecting your business can ease your fears.

Action Steps:

- » Maintain a healthy level of skepticism toward questionable invoices. Hire a lawyer when necessary.
- » Open a separate consumer credit card to pay business expenses.
- » Keep your online credentials secure. Use a password manager and install anti-malware software.
- » Work with an independent insurance agent to set up business and personal liability policies.

RULE 29

Strengthen Your Business's Weakest Links

As an owner of an Internet business, it is necessary to rely on different products and services from other companies in order to run your business. You will need a web-hosting company, content management system software like WordPress or Drupal, and possibly an email marketing provider like MailChimp (www.MailChimp.com) or Aweber (www.aweber.com) in order to manage your email list. You will need payment processing services like PayPal and Stripe. If you are a publisher, you will need to rely on an ad-network like Google AdSense (www.google.com/adsense). If you sell digital products, you may need to make use of an ordering and delivery service like Gumroad (www.gumroad.com). Regardless of what type of Internet business you build, it is important to recognize how many different companies you will be dependent upon to run your business.

Identifying Single Points of Failure

While other companies can provide incredibly powerful tools and services for you to build your business, it is important to recognize that they are not perfect and can actually be prone to failure. The companies that offer you services like web-hosting and payment processing also have the right to stop doing business with you whenever they want, unless you have signed a contract with them. This can be a dangerous proposition if you are totally reliant on one company for a critical component of your business. What would happen if your payment provider decided they did not want to accept money on your behalf anymore? What would happen if the web-server that hosts your website crashed? What would you do if the ad-network that generates the vast majority of your revenue kicks you off their network? These worst case scenarios do happen to entrepreneurs on a regular basis, so it is important to be prepared.

By relying only on one company for a component of your business, like payment processing or web-hosting, you create a single point of failure that is completely out of your control. While it is inevitable that these single points of failure will exist within your business, identifying them and having a plan B in place if something were to go terribly wrong is important. This means having an account set up with one of the company's competitors and having an action plan to make a quick switch over to the competitor if the first company is having issues.

For example, I rely both on SendGrid (www.sendgrid.com) and Amazon SES (aws.amazon.com/ses) for email delivery. In the event that one of them is having major issues, I can quickly switch over to the other provider. I also accept payments for all of my company's products and services through both Stripe and PayPal, so if either of these companies decided that they did not want to process payments for me anymore, my customers would be able to continue to order my products and services.

Redundancy Matters in Large Businesses

While having your website down or not being able to accept orders for a couple of days when you are first getting started might not be a big issue, these types of things become much more important when your company starts to grow and operate at scale. It is not a big deal if a website that generates $10 per day in revenue is down for a couple of days, but it is a big deal if a company that generates $2,500 per day in revenue is down for a couple of days. When your company expands, that business interruption insurance policy may come in handy so you still get paid in the event of a major issue that prevents customers from accessing your website.

As an online entrepreneur, get ahead of the game by recognizing where your business has its single points of failure before your website goes down. Have some prevention measures in place. If the web-server that hosts your site has some major issue and the web-hosting company cannot get your site back up, you are basically out of business until they can figure out what went wrong. For this reason, it is really important to select a well-respected hosting company from the start, regularly create backups of your websites, and have a secondary hosting option waiting in the wings if there is a problem with your web-host. My network of financial news websites receives anywhere from 2 million to 3 million page views each month. If the dedicated servers that host these websites are down for a day, I am out anywhere from $1,500 to $2,500 in lost ad-revenue and email sign-ups. For this reason, I create weekly backups of all of my websites using ManageWP (www.managewp.com) and spread my websites across two different servers. If one of them were to fail, I could temporarily move the sites from that server to my other dedicated server using the weekly backup and only have, at most, a few hours of downtime.

While these worst case scenarios tend to be rare, you should still plan ahead for them. By knowing which companies are capable of shutting down your business if they do not work or decide to stop doing business with you, you can have a ready-to-go plan B in the event that a worst case scenario does occur.

Action Steps:

- Identify the single points of failure within your business.
- Develop an action plan for each potential worst-case scenario that could interrupt your ability to do business.
- Secure your plan B options: secondary web-hosts, content management systems, payment processing services, etc.

RULE 30

Fail, Quit, and Regroup

While I have had a few successes with my Internet business, I have also started quite a few things that failed. I created a shopping comparison website for audio books called Audiobooktopia that I shutdown after determining there was no profitable way to market it. I created a public database of press releases that never gained any traction because it failed to solve anyone's problems. I started a WordPress performance optimization service called WP Mechanic that gained some good initial traction, but I quickly stopped marketing it after realizing how much work it would be to provide the service. These businesses initially looked like they were worth trying, but they did not work out so I made the decision to quit doing them to focus on other ideas that had more potential.

You may have heard the saying, "winners never quit and quitters never win." This saying, for entrepreneurs, is categorically wrong. The truth is that winners decide to quit things on a regular basis when they recognize that what they are doing does not work. Winners know their time is valuable and will not continue investing time and energy into things that they know are unrecoverable failures. There is a quote that has been attributed to Albert Einstein, Rita Mae Brown and Benjamin Franklin that says, "insanity is doing the same thing over and over and expecting different results." If you are doing something that is clearly not working in your business, you should not keep doing it just because you are determined not to give up.

A Temporary Setback, or Total Failure?

The key to understanding when to quit is knowing the differences between a temporary setback in your business and the fundamental failure of your business model. Seth Godin speaks about this issue in his book, The Dip. He wrote, "The Cul-de-Sac [French for "dead end"]...is a situation where you work and work and work and nothing much changes." If you have a lot of work ahead of you, but see shimmers of light at the end of the tunnel, you should probably push forward through the dip. However, if you cannot find one customer to purchase your product or service and see no clear path to getting your first customer, take it as a sign that it is time to do something different. If you work on your business for an extended period of time and see absolutely no progress, give yourself permission to quit and try something else.

Shiny Object Syndrome

If you are simply more excited about a different project than the one you are working on now, you might be suffering from shiny object syndrome. You see a shiny new business idea far off in the distance and decide that you want that idea more than the business you are working on now. While you know all of the strengths, weaknesses, and fine details about the business you have, you will not know the less than desirable parts of the new business that you want to start simply because you have not started it yet. If you keep switching from business idea to business idea because of shiny object syndrome, you will end up with a collection of half-finished, not-so-shiny businesses and nothing to show for yourself. At some point, your current business was shiny and new. Do not give up on your current business because you see something new that you might be interested in. The decision to quit your current business is a serious one, only do it when you believe you have exhausted your ideas about how to make it work.

Regrouping after Failure

I am not saying that you should give up the goal of creating an Internet business or on your dreams of regaining freedom over your time and financial independence when you decide it is time to make a significant change or quit working your current business. What it does mean is that you should quit the specific strategies and business plans that are not working for you. Fundamentally re-evaluate your target market, your product, and your marketing strategy. Maybe you picked a market of customers who are not willing to buy. Maybe you are unable to reach your target market on a cost effective basis. Maybe your product or service does not actually solve anyone's problems. Identify which part of your business is not working without regard to how much work you have already put into that part of your .product. If it needs to go, it needs to go. You may just need to change your marketing strategy or find a different market for your product. If so, make the necessary changes. You may decide you need to scrap your entire product and start over with a different target market. Do what you need to do. It is better to start over now and set aside all the work you have done than to continue on a failed path.

Remember that the most successful entrepreneurs in the world have faced failure, quit what was not working for them, and regrouped along the way. Steve Jobs was fired from Apple in 1985. Bill Gates' first company, Traf-O-Data, failed because he and his partners could not make the product work. Richard Branson was almost jailed while building his first business, Student Magazine, for publishing remedies to sexually transmitted diseases. Entrepreneurs, by nature, try out a lot of things that do not work. You are going to fail at some point and have to quit. Consider the Japanese proverb, "Fall down seven times, stand up eight." By quitting, you free yourself from something that you know is not going to work so that you can work on something that has a better chance at success. Stand up and reach out for what comes next.

Action Steps:

- » Recognize that failing, quitting, and regrouping are natural parts of becoming a successful entrepreneur.
- » Avoid shiny object syndrome. Do not quit your current business just because you think that a different business might be a better option.
- » Know when to continue with your business and when to quit.

Growing Your Business

RULE 31

If You Build It, They Won't Come

Building an Internet business is not the entrepreneurial version of *Field of Dreams*. If you build it, there is no guarantee that anyone will come to your website. Do not assume that people will buy your company's product or service just because you make it available online. When you build a brick-and-mortar business on a busy street corner or in a crowded shopping mall, customers will naturally wander into your store. When you build an Internet business, you are located in the digital equivalent of a lone storefront in the middle of the countryside. You have to actively convince potential customers to come into your store and buy your company's products and services.

One of the most common sins committed by entrepreneurs is spending too much time developing their product or service and not nearly enough time marketing it. Marketing cannot be an afterthought. As you are building, you should begin marketing. In the world of Internet business, this means creating an email list for your product's launch and getting your marketing website ready. Put up a splash page on your site that invites people to get more information about your product. Send potential customers to your splash page through blogs, guest posts on related websites, interviews on podcasts, and other types of online advertising. When it comes time to launch your product, you will be able to send marketing emails to hundreds of potential customers who have already expressed interest in your product.

Marketing Mondays

In order to ensure that you adequately balance the amount of work you put into product development and marketing, I suggest you take one day each week and devote it only to marketing activities. This strategy is often referred to as Marketing Mondays. On the day of the week you choose, you will commit to working solely on tasks that are related to marketing and selling your product.

Here are some activities to consider for your Marketing Mondays:

- Create an opt-in form to collect email addresses of potential customers.
- Work on the website you will use to market your product.
- Contact related blogs and offer to write a guest post on their website.
- Contact related podcasts and offer to be a guest on their show. Prepare a few topics to suggest when you send your email.
- Talk with people on social media platforms and discussion forums about the problems your product or service can solve.
- Write blog posts about your upcoming product or service and promote them through Reddit, Twitter, Facebook, Pinterest and other relevant social media platforms.
- Research different ways that you can advertise your product or service.

Identify New Marketing Channels

After your product has launched, your next goal will be to develop a process to regularly test different marketing strategies and customer acquisition methods to ensure that you have a diversified set of web traffic sources. Ideally, you will have somewhere between five and ten sources of traffic that regularly send web traffic and new customers to your business. Search engines and social media sites can be sources of new potential customers, but they should not be your primary methods of customer acquisition.

Acquiring a variety of traffic for your business is a matter of persevering through trial and error.

Try to diversify your traffic sources: you should not have one traffic source that is responsible for more than 25% of your new customers. For example, my investment newsletter business, Analyst Ratings Network (www.analystratings.net), receives sign-ups from Bing Finance, StockTwits, our Android/iPhone App, Yahoo Finance, Twitter, Google AdWords, co-registration advertising, Google

Finance, and email list swaps. It has taken three years to develop these traffic streams. While there is no guarantee they will continue to send new customers to my business, I will continue to attract new customers even if one of these traffic sources disappeared. But brace yourself: acquiring a variety of traffic for your business is a matter of persevering through trial and error.

The vast majority of the marketing strategies that you try will be ineffective, but every now and then you will find a profitable way to acquire new customers. A marketing strategy is effective if it costs less to acquire a customer from that particular source than the lifetime value of your typical customer. Once you have found something that works, do everything you can to maximize the flow of new customers from that traffic stream, whether that means increasing your advertising spending or publishing more content to that particular platform. When you are first getting started, I recommend trying as many as a dozen different strategies for a couple of months, then honing in on the strategies that are working well. After your company is up and running, continue to test one new marketing strategy every month.

If you are unsure of which marketing strategies to test for your business, here are several you could try:

- Purchase or rent an email list of executives who work in your target market.
- Start a pay-per-click advertising campaign through Google AdWords.
- Have conversations with people in your market on social media sites.
- Launch a direct mail campaign to individuals in your target market.
- Ask owners of websites in your target market if you can do a guest post on their website.
- Create an app relevant to your target market and put it on the AppStore and the Google Play Store.
- Target category-specific search engines like Google Images, Google News or Google Finance.
- Create videos about your topic on YouTube.
- Buy advertisements on websites and in magazines relevant to your target market.

Of course, these are just a few of the many ways that

entrepreneurs can attract customers to their online businesses. The key is to try a lot of different things and see what works for your particular business.

Action Steps:

» Spend one day per week doing marketing tasks while you are developing your product.
» Identify five different marketing strategies that you can try to attract new customers.
» Determine whether a particular marketing strategy is successful for you.

RULE 32

Results-Driven Advertising

There are two broad categories of advertising: advertising for brand-building purposes and advertising for direct-marketing purposes. Brand advertisements attempt to keep a specific company in a consumer's mind the next time they go to make a purchase.

A great example of a brand building advertisement is the commercial series that the Coca-Cola Company puts on TV featuring polar bears that drink Coke.[2] This series of commercials contains an entertaining minute of video featuring playful polar bears drinking Coke products in hopes of cementing the Coca-Cola brand in the mind of the consumer. Notice there is no call-to-action at the end of commercial telling people to drive to their local grocery store and purchase a twelve-pack of coke. Success rates for brand-building advertisements are generally difficult to measure unless you are a very large company that can afford to do focus groups and market surveys.

Examples of Brand Advertising Include:

» Billboards
» Magazine Ads that Feature a Brand
» Product Placements
» Promotional Productions Such as T-Shirts and Pens
» Television Commercials without a Clear Call-To-Action
» Display Advertisements on the Web

Direct Marketing

Advertising using direct marketing asks the viewer to take immediate action after watching. Direct marketing advertisements may attempt

[2] "Coke 2012 Commercial: Catch" (https://www.youtube.com/watch?v= S2nBBMbjS8w)

to provide more information if the viewer proceeds to their online form, calls a phone number to set up an appointment, makes a purchase, or orders a product through an online shopping cart. Direct marketing ads exist solely for the purpose of getting your potential customer to take a specific action. The quintessential example of direct marketing is late-night infomercials. They do not attempt to promote the brand of the company selling the product. Their only goal is to get you to call their phone number and order their product. The results of direct marketing ads are heavily measured and placements of these advertisements are quickly discontinued if they are not found to be profitable. Direct Marketing ads are frequently tweaked and tested to improve their performance.

Examples of Direct Marketing Ads Include:

» Cost-Per-Action Advertising (Affiliate Marketing)
» Coupons
» Direct Mail
» Email Marketing
» Infomercials
» Pay-Per-Click Advertising such as Google AdWords

You Can't Afford Brand Advertising

As a small Internet business, brand building is not in your budget. Brand advertising requires the purchase of expensive television commercials, billboards and magazine ads. Think about a typical congressional campaign. Each congressperson represents about 800,000 people. In order to create an image or brand, winning campaigns will typically spend about $1.7 million per election cycle.[3] You will be a small part of a very large market and you simply will not be able to afford to get your brand in the minds of a significant part of your market without a substantial amount of capital. Running ads without knowing if they are successful is impossible for a one-person Internet business. You can still do brand building activities, but do not plan to put a lot of money into expensive brand-building advertisements.

[3] Terbush, Jon. "What It Costs to Win a Congressional Election". The Week, 11 Mar. 2013. Web, 23 Apr. 2014. <www.bit.ly/1iwqlLc>

Measure the Results of Every Ad-Buy

Instead, spend your precious advertising dollars on things that can be directly measured so you know if you are getting a return on the investment of your ad spend. Whether you do pay-per-click advertising through Google AdWords, purchase the ability to send an advertising email to someone's mailing list, or use direct placement on someone's website, you should always measure how much it costs for you to get a customer from every area where you are advertising. If you spend $500 to place an advertisement on someone's website for a month and you get five customers from that advertisement, your cost per customer acquisition is $100.

You will probably try a lot of different advertising networks and strategies. If you find a method of advertising that is close to breaking even, it is worth continuing to tweak your ads to see if you can make the campaign profitable. You can use Google Analytics (www.google.com/analytics) to track sales. Also, check the content management system and shopping cart software you use, these may contain the ability to track the origins of your sales.

Types of Advertising for Your Internet Business

The types of advertising that will work best for your particular Internet business will largely depend on your target market. If you are building an e-commerce store, Google Product Ads and Amazon PPC would be a good place to start. If you are building an audience through an email list, you might consider doing co-registration advertising. If you are creating a niche product or service for a particular industry, you could find websites with content for that market and buy banner ad placements on their website from the website owner. If you are trying to build an audience around a particular topic and hope to sell your customers information products like e-books and membership sites, you might want to focus on Facebook ads.

Focus your time on establishing connections and building relationships.

With all of the advertising possibilities available to Internet business entrepreneurs, keep in mind that when you are trying to establish yourself as an expert and create a community surrounding your content, you should focus your time on establishing connections and building relationships with people in your community. Only start advertising when you have a product or a service to sell.

Action Steps:

- » Identify which types of direct marketing advertisements would work for your online business.
- » Determine how you are going to track sales from specific advertising channels to measure the results of your ad-buy.
- » Test and tweak your "almost breaking even" advertisements to make that ad campaign profitable.

RULE 33

Go Where the People Are

There are a number of people who offer courses on specific advertising platforms and marketing strategies. Perry Marshall will teach you how to grow your business with Google AdWords. Jon McIntyre will teach you how to talk to your target market using email marketing. John Lee Dumas will tell you to start a podcast and Pat Flynn will simply tell you to, "Be everywhere!" Any number of entrepreneurs can teach you to advertise on Facebook and Twitter. The problem with following the advice in courses that teach you how to follow a single marketing strategy is that the best way to acquire new customers varies substantially from business to business depending on your target audience. If you have a business-to-business product, chances are Facebook is not going to be your best marketing channel. If you have an older audience, then podcasts might not be the right choice. If your audience is predominately male, Pinterest is probably not your best bet. The key to identifying which marketing strategies are going to work the best for your business is to identify your target market and find the places where they congregate online. Put simply: go where the people are.

Create an Avatar of Your Ideal Customer

Think back to Rule 11 and your target audience. Remember the questions you asked yourself and the process of narrowing down your ideal customer? A common recommendation when trying to develop online marketing strategies is to create a fictional character, called an avatar, which epitomizes your typical customer. By creating an avatar, you will have a better idea of who you are marketing to and in many ways, can get inside the mind of your target audience.

For Analyst Ratings Network (www.analystratings.net), our avatar is named Bill. He is about fifty years old. He is married, is a homeowner, and has some money to invest in the stock market. He is not sure whose advice he should listen to when picking his own stocks, though he likes to do this himself. He can live just about anywhere in the United States or Canada and loves to keep up with the day-to-day news in the stock market. For GoGo Photo Contest (www.gogophotocontest.com), our avatar is named Kristie. She is about forty years old and can live anywhere in the United States. She volunteers or works at an animal shelter and will do anything for the welfare of animals. She is underpaid and has limited resources to help the animals she is so passionate about.

Where Does Your Audience Congregate?

Once you have identified your customer avatar, you will want to start talking to people who resemble your avatar and identify what they have in common. What websites do they visit? What magazines do they read? Do they use search engines? Are they members of any non-profit organizations? Are they members of any online communities? Are there directories that contain listings of members of your target market?

After talking to several people who are part of your target audience, you will start to identify certain common threads between them. Perhaps they subscribe to the same magazine or visit the same websites on a regular basis. They might be on a common email list. If your target audience works in a specific profession, there may be online directories that contain a list of potential target customers.

After you have identified what ties members of your target market together, you need to find a way to get to them in the places where they congregate. If your target market is part of an online community, join that community and participate in its on-going conversation. If your target audience subscribes to a common publication or visits a common website, buy an advertisement in that magazine or on that website to put your business in their view. If your audience uses Google to get information about the product or services you offer, consider a Google AdWords campaign or some search engine optimization work.

For Analyst Ratings Network, my target audience frequently visits investment research websites like Benzinga.com, TheStreet.com and 247WallStreet.com. In order to gain access to my audience on these websites, I have set up a co-registration advertising campaign so that whenever someone signs up for their email lists, they will see an advertisement to sign-up for my email list as well. When my target audience discusses stocks on social networks like StockTwits and Twitter, I participated in those social media conversations by publishing stock ratings to those platforms. When they use Google to search for things like "stock recommendations" and "stock ratings," I have set up a small AdWords campaign to catch these email addresses.

I wish I could say that every new entrepreneur should promote their business with Facebook, email marketing, or Google AdWords, but it is not that simple. While there are courses that will teach you to advertise using a specific platform, there are probably no courses that will teach you to target your specific audience. You will need to do the work yourself. Then, you will need to find a way to get where they can see you. Go where the people are.

Action Steps:

» Develop an avatar of your typical customer.

» Talk to three to five people in your target market about your business.

» Identify as many ways as possible to reach your target audience.

RULE 34

Don't Rely on Social Media, SEO, or the Tech Press to Market Your Business

New entrepreneurs usually underestimate how large a task customer acquisition can be. Unfortunately, they also tend to believe a variety of myths about marketing. For instance, the myth that they only need to get their website featured on TechCrunch in order to acquire a large number customers or the myth that their product will go viral on Facebook or Twitter and that they will not need to do much marketing. They may even believe that they merely need to do some basic search engine optimization work and Google will send them all of the customers that they need. Do not be the entrepreneur who falls for these myths. Marketing your product or service is a large and challenging task that will take as much time and effort as building the product itself.

The Tech Press Won't Send You Customers

For quite a while, entrepreneurs believed that their ticket to getting a large number of new users was to have their business featured on the front page of Hacker News, TechCrunch, Re/Code or Mashable. Now, if any major members of the technology press were to cover your business, you would get a large wave of web traffic for a few days, but that is about all you will get for the media coverage. Getting featured on popular technology blogs rarely leads to a large influx of new users or customers. Most people who read the major tech sites are just browsing and are not actually that interested in your company's product or service. They are probably not your target audience, either. Do your potential customers read TechCrunch and related sites? Consider your avatar. The tech press should not be the marketing channel that you pursue. Do not expect that having your website featured on another popular website will drive a meaningful number of customers to your business.

SEO Is Not (Always) Reliable

While SEO can be one of the traffic strategies you employ, I do not think it should be your primary customer acquisition strategy because you have very little control over how much web traffic Google sends you. Google has a complex algorithm it uses to decide which websites will rank in top positions for any given keyword and the algorithm changes on a regular basis. If you rely too heavily on getting traffic from Google, your business is at significant risk. Consider how many publishers got hammered in the search rankings in 2011 and 2012 when Google announced the various iterations of the "Panda" and "Penguin" updates. Many publishers saw the volume of traffic that Google sent them decline by 70% overnight. I was one of those publishers. I had been successfully marketing Audible(R)'s audiobook subscription service through search engine optimization and lost $7,000 in monthly revenue overnight. After the first few "Panda" updates, my SEO-driven affiliate marketing efforts were no longer effective. I have since moved on to other businesses that have much more diversified sources of web traffic.

"Going Viral" Can't Be Replicated

The vast majority of content designed to go viral never gets any traction. You might spend several thousand dollars to create a video designed to go viral and end up getting only a few hundred views on YouTube. You should certainly be active on platforms that have the capacity to go viral, such as Facebook, Twitter, and YouTube, but your marketing strategy cannot be dependent upon having your content going viral. Even if you were to have one piece of content hit, there would be no guarantee that the next viral piece of content you create will generate the same amount of traction.

Do yourself a favor and do not believe these myths. Instead, do the hard work to regularly identify and test out new marketing channels. Your marketing will not be as glamorous as getting your company featured on a popular news website as going viral, but you will develop sustainable and scalable ways to attract new customers to your business.

RULE 35

Own Your Customer List

During the last decade, there has been a trend for online entrepreneurs to build their businesses on top of various platforms offered by web companies, such as Apple (iTunes, AppStore), eBay, Facebook, Google (Search, YouTube, Google Play Store), and Twitter. This has not always been a successful process. Several years ago, many believed that the path to building a growing Internet business was to sell products on eBay. This worked until eBay changed its price structure and policies so that many small sellers could not make a profit within eBay's ecosystems. Between 2008 and 2011, many entrepreneurs were working to build the next great Twitter client or Facebook application. These businesses gained some traction until Twitter decided it wanted to own its client experience and Facebook clamped down on the ability of third party apps to post on behalf of users. The latest trend has been to create smartphone apps on Apple's AppStore and Google's Play Store. There have been dozens of cases where developers had their apps removed from the AppStore for arbitrary and subjective reasons, such as AppGratis.

Don't Rely On Someone Else's Ecosystem to Communicate with Your Customers

When you build a business inside an established ecosystem such as iTunes, YouTube, or Facebook, there are benefits to tapping into an established base of users. However, you place your business at significant risk. By piggybacking off of a major company's platform, your business only continues to exist as long as it suits the needs of your host company. When the platform owner decides that your business is not needed, you are out of luck. When a large company you are working with makes a change to their platform that hurts your business, you have no process for recourse or even the ability to appeal to the company's sense of reason. They have no business relationship with you. You are just one of the thousands of minor partners and are easily replaceable.

Your future ability to generate income is based on the relationship you have with your customers and your ability to communicate with them. If you are dependent upon another company's platform to communicate with your customers, they are not really your customers. If the platform suddenly changes, you may lose your ability to communicate with your customers and you are basically out of business.

A while back, many companies invested in building large followings using Facebook Fan Pages. Facebook then changed the rules and decided that it would start charging page owners to promote posts to their followers. The NBA's Dallas Mavericks were asked to pay as much as $3,000 to send a single message to their audience on Facebook.[4] If you have built your audience on a Facebook Fan page only to find out that you must now pay a significant sum of money just to reach them, your ability to generate future income is greatly hampered. So how do you connect permanently and securely with your customers?

Build an Email List of Your Customers

Avoid these ecosystem dependency issues by getting the email addresses of all your customers. Do not rely on having a large following on social media platforms or a bunch of users who have your app installed to communicate with your customers. By having an email list, you have the ability to contact all of your customers in the future regardless of the specific platforms you utilize to build your customer base. While social networks can come and go, people's email addresses rarely ever change. Nobody is building an audience on MySpace anymore, but if you were able to get the email addresses of the people who liked your MySpace page ten years ago, there is a good chance you could still communicate with them. If you have the email addresses of all of your customers, you will always be able to communicate with them even if Apple, Facebook, Google or

[4] Fitzgerald, Britney. "Mark Cuban Fed Up with Facebook, Plans to Take His Brand Pages Elsewhere" The Huffington Post: Tech. November 13, 2012. <http://www.huffingtonpost.com/2012/11/13/mark-cuban-facebook _n_2122704.html>

Twitter decides that they do not want you anymore, or they want to charge you to use their platforms to connect to customers. Use your email list to tell your customers about the next project that you are working on or a related product or service that you are marketing. Your ongoing relationship with your customers should be between you and your customers: big tech companies should not have the ability to hurt that relationship.

If you currently rely on another company's platform to communicate with your customers, I recommend creating opt-in pages where your users can get some sort of bonus content in exchange for giving you their email address. If you have a large audience on Facebook or Twitter, you might create a free report or a special interview and require the user to provide their email address in exchange for access. If you are publishing books on Amazon, liberally include links back to your website and create a bonus that requires an email opt-in to access. If you have customers who use your iPhone or Android apps, consider providing additional features to users who provide you with their email address.

Action Steps:

» Maintain an active email list of your customers so that you can communicate with them in the future.

» Determine what percent of your audience currently comes from large web company platforms.

» Use bonuses and opt-in forms to collect the email addresses of your audiences who know you via a larger company's platform.

RULE 36

Show Credibility with Social Proof

When you are looking to make a purchase in the brick-and-mortar business world, there are usually some clues as to whether or not you are buying from a reputable retailer. If the store has an empty parking lot in the middle of the day and the building is dirty and unkempt, you have good reason to be suspicious. If the product you are considering does not look like it is supposed to, or if the salesperson is being especially pushy, you know something is not quite right. It is much more difficult to tell whether an online business is reputable or not. Just about anyone can have a professional website designed and have some good marketing copy written, but that does not tell you whether or not the company is reputable. Scam artists have every incentive to make their websites look as professional as possible, so it is important to show your potential customers the legitimacy of your company through a variety of social proofs.

Get Reviews and Testimonials

One of the best ways to show your credibility is to get reviews and testimonials. Around 70% of Americans read product reviews before making a purchase so it is especially important to showcase the reviews and testimonials of your company's product or service.[5] An easy way to get testimonials for your product is to ask the people who have already bought your product for a three-to-four sentence testimonial about their experience with your business. You would be surprised at how many people are willing to provide testimonials for products and services, especially if they have had a good experience. When listing the testimonials and reviews that

[5] Ante, Spencer. "Amazon: Turning Consumer Opinions into Gold". *Business Week*. 15 Oct. 2009. Web. 14 Mar 2014.

you receive on your website, include the customer's full name, the company they work for, links to their social media profiles and a picture if possible. Testimonials about your product are much more credible if a potential customer is able to lookup the person who wrote the review and identify that they are a real person.

If your product is relatively new or has not launched yet, consider reaching out to influential people in your target market. These are people who have blogs, podcasts, or a following on YouTube. Offer to send them one of your products or provide them access to your service and see if they would be willing to do a review of your product on their website. People often search for product names followed by the word review, for example: "GoGo Photo Contest Review." If you can get other websites to review your product and show up in those searches, you will boost the credibility of your business.

Using Social Media

You can also demonstrate credibility by having an active presence on Facebook and Twitter. If you have a few hundred followers on each platform, potential customers know that there are other people who have demonstrated a real interest in what you have to offer.

By regularly posting on your Facebook Page and Twitter account, you show that you are still in business and are actively engaged with your customers. You can also demonstrate this with an up-to-date news section on your website. Many companies make the mistake of creating a news section on their website and then forgetting to update it. The news section is not news if you have not posted anything in the last 18 months. If you decide to have a news section on your website, make sure to update it at least once per month.

Show Off Your Real-World Presence

Finally, show that there are real people behind your company. List the members of your team, along with their job titles, pictures, links to social media profiles, and email addresses on your website. This will show that you and your team are accessible and open. You are not trying to hide behind the veil of anonymity that the Internet can provide. Also, include your physical address on your website along with a phone number so that people know they can contact you. If your company has office space, put a picture of the building on your "About" page. By proudly showing off your team members along with your company's location and real world contact information, your potential customers will know you are not just an anonymous website or worse, a scam trying to take people's money.

Action Steps:

- » Collect reviews and testimonials from your customers and place them on your website.
- » Contact influential people in your target market and ask them if they would be willing to review your product or service.
- » Create and actively maintain social media profiles and news updates to interact with your customers.
- » Showcase your team members, physical address, phone number, and other pertinent company information on your website.

RULE 37

Always Be Testing

The process of acquiring customers for your business is a long road with many exits, several roadblocks, and a few strategically-placed billboards that advertise your company and its products along the way. At one end of the road are potential customers who don't know that your company exists yet. In order to become a satisfied customer, they need to start down your road, become aware of your business through advertising, and not get stuck in any roadblocks along the way or take an exit off in the direction of another company before they reach their destination: your business. You have the ability to control how your advertising affects customers and can learn how to identify and eliminate road blocks as they appear by testing your marketing material.

Identify and eliminate road blocks by testing your marketing material.

Knowing your target market will allow you to provide better content and more user-friendly options, increasing your chances of turning your website visitors into your customers. When designing the marketing for your business, it is not always clear which components of your marketing material will do better than variations of that same piece of marketing material. You may ask yourself: should your call-to-action button color be blue or orange? Should you include a video tour of your product on the landing page? Will charging $9.97 produce more sales than charging $10? You can make sure that you get the right answers to these questions by running a split-test, sometimes called an A/B test.

A split-test is the process of showing a random half of your users one style, layout, and content and the other half a version of the original with one or more modifications. Over a period of time, you can review the data and determine which version performs better. For example, say you want to determine whether or not changing the text on an email opt-in button from, "Subscribe Now" to, "Sign-Up Now (Free)" will increase opt-in rates to an email list. You would alternate the button text between every other visitor who sees the opt-in form. After you get enough sign-ups for the result of the test to be statically significant, for instance, after 200 total sign-ups, you would see which of the two versions of the button got higher opt-in rates. If you showed, "Subscribe Now" to 2,500 visitors and got 90 sign-ups and, "Sign-Up Now (Free)" to another set of 2,500 visitors and got 110 sign-ups, you would know that, "Sign-Up Now (Free)" is the optimal text to use on your opt-in form because its opt-in rates are 22% better than the original text.

After reviewing the results from that first test, you could test any number of other parts of your opt-in form: the positioning of the opt-in form, the heading, the copy, what information you collect, the font, or the colors you are using. Imagine that you did a series of ten different tests to find your optimal opt-in button. As you review your data, you see that seven of them showed no significant difference, but three of them improved opt-in rates by 15%. Your discovery would not be a cumulative benefit of those three successful tests: 45% = (15% + 15% + 15%). The benefits of split-tests are multiplicative. By improving opt-in rates 15% three different times, your sign-up rate would actually improve by 52% (1.15 * 1.15 * 1.15).

What Should You Test?

You can test just about anything on your website to determine whether or not changing it will increase the rate at which your customers sign-up. You should certainly spend a lot of time testing your value proposition. What do my customers get for their money? What features and benefits will encourage them to buy? Ideally, you will be running split tests at every step of the journey that your potential customers take to find out what drives them to your website and keeps them there. However, you will want to test out the following as a start:

- Your value proposition
- A variety of different traffic sources
- The initial ad-copy that sends a user to your registration page

- The landing page
- Your auto-responder series
- Marketing emails used for communicating with prospects
- The sales page: the headline and marketing copy, font, color, layout
- Call-to-action button: text, size, location, color, number of buttons
- Order Form: type and amount of information
- Pricing: one-time vs. recurring, discounts, final cost, payment methods

After a while, you will start to see diminishing returns on your tests and many tests simply will not work as well as the copy you already have, but the few tests that do perform well will make a significant difference in your business and help you create your optimal approach to keeping your customers. If you are looking for an extensive list of different things you can split-test, Optimizely, a website optimization software company, has recently published a list of 71 different things you can split test on your website.[6]

How to Test: Tools for Split-Testing

You might be thinking: well, that sounds great, but I have no idea how to run a split test. In the past, you had to hire a software developer to implement split tests on your website and track the results. Fortunately, there are now software tools like Optimizely (www.optimizely.com) and Visual Website Optimizer (www.visualwebsiteoptimizer.com) that make setting up split-tests on your website dead simple. Optimizely and Visual Website Optimizer provide point-and-click tools that will allow you to create variations of your website, automatically serve them to different users, and track the results to see which variation produces your desired outcome.

Split Testing in Action

When I first started my investment newsletter business, I had a single opt-in box at the bottom of each article and was getting between 500 and 800 visitors per month depending on traffic. After running three years of tests on the various opt-in mechanisms I use to collect email addresses on my website, I am now regularly getting

[6] http://blog.optimizely.com/2013/04/30/71-things-to-ab-test/.

5,000 to 8,000 email sign-ups per month. Granted, the amount of web-traffic I am getting has increased by 250%, but the opt-in rate to my newsletter has increased by more than 400% since I first started collecting email addresses. That means there are four times as many people getting my free email newsletter, four times as many people receiving marketing material for my company's premium products, four times as many people ending up on one of my landing pages, and four times as many people buying products and services from my company. And that turns into four times as much revenue for my business. That is real money.

Action Steps:

- » Setup split-testing software on your website
- » Identify ten different components of your customer acquisition process to test over several months
- » Start your first split test today!

RULE 38

Use the Three Keys of Revenue Growth

Many entrepreneurs believe that the only way to generate more revenue in their business is to get more customers. While this is certainly true, there are two other key factors that contribute to revenue growth that entrepreneurs often ignore. When combined with customer acquisition, I call these factors the three keys to revenue growth. The second key is to increase product sales or the frequency of those sales to your existing customers. The third key is to make sure you keep your churn rate low by convincing existing customers to stick around and continue buying from you.

Gaining New Customers

If you have a hard time making any of your marketing channels profitable, or if you have only one very good marketing channel, you know that getting new customers is not something that you can force or just sit back and wish for. Your ability to attract new customers may be limited because of your current approach. You may have created some basic marketing and hoped that more customers will show up and buy your product or service. Unfortunately, hope is not an effective marketing strategy.

Attracting new customers must be an ever-active pursuit.

Attracting new customers to your business must be an ever-active pursuit. You should regularly try out new advertising strategies and marketing channels. Do not be afraid to ask your customers for referrals. This can be simple as asking your customers whether or not they know anyone else who might benefit from your product or service. If you already have a productive marking channel, you should look at why it is working and see how you can maximize the amount of leads that this channel can send you. If there is a potential audience who is not aware of your product or service, you could consider acquiring a list of people in your target market and doing a direct mail or email campaign. If you want to get new customers for your business, you need to go out and get them through strategic and systematic marketing work.

Selling More to Your Existing Customers

The second key to generating revenue growth is to sell more products to your existing customers or sell your products to your existing customers more often. If your product or service can be purchased by your customers multiple times, set up an email auto-responder series that encourages your customers to buy your product again. Companies that make physical products, such as vitamin supplements, will try to make you use more of their products with recommended usage amounts and artificial expiration dates.

In the world of Internet business, you can apply these marketing techniques as well. For example, in my press release distribution business, I could encourage my customers to publish a press release every two weeks in order to get the maximum benefit from their promotional efforts. This way they continue to use my service in a way that benefits them, but at a rate or frequency that is more profitable to me. You can also encourage your customers to re-order your product or service by selling it on a time-limited basis. For the web-based investment research software my company sells, called RatingsDB, customers do not buy the product once and get lifetime access to the service. They buy a twelve-month license and have to renew after a year. Instead of just getting paid once to access the service, my customers will pay for the service every year as long as they continue to use the product.

The other way to sell more to your existing customers is to create new products or add-on products and services beyond what you are already selling to them. With Analyst Ratings Network, we initially had one product: our premium daily newsletter. We had customers ask us how to use the information in the newsletter, so we created a $39 investment guide called *The Trader's Guide to Equities Research*. With Lightning Releases, we had customers who asked for help when writing their press releases in addition to having us distribute it, so we created an add-on purchase where customers could have us write their release for them for an additional $99. As you sell your product or service, look for ways to create additional products and services to sell to your customers. Their feedback can help you develop something that is related to what you are already selling them now.

Keeping Your Existing Customers Around

The third and final key to growing your company's revenue is to make sure you are keeping your customers around. The rate at which your customers cancel your service over a specific period of time is called your churn rate. This measurement is especially important if you have a client base that buys from you on a regular basis or a product that generates recurring income. If you see a sudden spike in your churn rate, you know that there is a problem somewhere within your business.

If customers are canceling their subscriptions or services at a higher rate than they had previously, find out why. You should not take it personally when someone decides to stop being your customer, because no one is going to be your customer forever. However, you should take the time to understand why they have decided to stop doing business with you so you can do a better job for your other customers and your future customers. The best way to do this is to send them a personal email, thank them for being a customer, and ask them why they are canceling your service. If you have the ability to track your customers' usage of your products, it is a good idea to see which customers are not using your product and see if you can re-engage them before they cancel your service. If you do recurring billing, you may find that customers do not always keep their payment methods up-to-date. If someone's payment fails to process properly, send them a personal email and try to get them to provide an up-to-date payment method.

If you want to maximize the amount of revenue your company makes, you need to leverage all three keys of revenue growth together. Attract new customers, maximize the life-time value of each of your customers, and do what you can to make sure your current customers stay with you.

Action Steps:

- » Ask your current customers for referrals.
- » Consider a direct mail or email marketing campaign to acquire new customers.
- » Look for add-on products and services that you can create and sell to your existing customers.
- » Measure your churn rate on a monthly basis.
- » Email your former customers to ask why they left.

RULE 39

Turn Over Stones

After you have built your Internet business and have been in business for a couple of years, there will be hidden and untapped revenue streams that your company could tap into if you knew they existed. Many business owners grow their company's revenue by raising their prices or selling their products and services to new customers, but they seldom go hunting for new potential revenue streams. Do not assume that your current methods of earning income are the only potential income streams that your business could have.

Look for ways to do things a little differently. Package your business's products and services in a fresh, new way and sell it to a new audience. Find a related product or service that you can sell to your existing base of customers. Seek out a new ad-network that will pay above average rates to market to your audience. Keep your eyes open and search for these hidden revenue streams. If you only focus on the day-to-day operations of your business, you will not be able to identify new sources of income. Finding these hidden revenue streams requires creative thinking, competitive research, and regularly trying out new ideas.

Identifying Hidden Revenue Streams

There have been several times during the history of American Consumer News, LLC where I have sought out and found hidden revenue streams that have added thousands of dollars in net profit to the company's bottom line. In 2010, I received an unsolicited email from a company that wanted to license the content from American Banking and Market News for use in research databases and various proprietary search tools. I receive a lot of pitches out of the blue from companies that want me to use their ad-network or submit content to my websites. I could have easily deleted this email along with the others as spam, but I did a little bit of research and talked to some of the companies that partner with them. Since there was no potential downside to my business, I decided to give them a shot. To this day, they pay my company approximately $3,000 per month in licensing fees to use our content. If I had not been open to new opportunities and dismissed their initial email as another spam message, I would have never uncovered this extra income in my revenue stream. When you are presented with an opportunity out of the blue, take a bit of time to give it a cursory evaluation before saying no reflexively.

If you do not receive regular offers yet, another great way to identify hidden revenue streams is to keep an eye on what your competitors are doing. Regularly check out your competitor's websites to learn about their new ideas in their company news, product announcements and marketing promotions. If they have an email list, sign-up and stay on it. That way, you will know how they are marketing to their customers and will be able to see if they are doing something that you should be doing as well. You should not be paranoid about what your competitors are doing, but do keep a healthy level of interest in their activities. If at all possible, become friends with entrepreneurs who are in your market space. Internet businesses are rarely a zero-sum game where a new customer for your company means someone else loses a customer, so you are not always in direct competition with other entrepreneurs in similar businesses.

Befriend Your Competitors

I have tried to maintain a healthy relationship with people from other companies who do financial reporting during the last several years and have received valuable suggestions and advice as a result. In early 2013, an acquaintance in my industry asked if I had thought about showing co-registration ads to people who sign-up for my email list. Prior to this conversation, new email subscribers had been sent to a thank you page telling them they would receive their first newsletter soon, so I decided to set up a co-registration advertising block below the thank you message to try it out. My company has earned more than $50,000 in co-registration commissions during the last twelve months using this small change on a thank you page that I thought, before I tried it out, had little advertising value. I was unable to uncover this particular income stream because I maintained a healthy relationship with other people in my industry and have kept a keen eye on what my competitors are doing.

Maximize Your Existing Revenue Streams

Finally, make your existing streams of revenue flow faster. Look for ways to maximize existing sources of web traffic and revenue on a regular basis. A while back, I had noticed that some of my Analyst Ratings Network subscribers were sharing our content on StockTwits and Twitter on a regular basis and were receiving healthy traffic back to our website as a result. In order to maximize these web traffic sources, I placed prominent StockTwits and Twitter share buttons on my website and in my newsletter. I also created StockTwits and Twitter accounts for Analyst Ratings Network and started publishing on those platforms directly. By seeing the potential of those two particular web traffic streams and maximizing our use of them, we were able to get an additional 500 new newsletter subscribers per month and currently get more than 2,000 additional unique visitors to our website each day the stock market is open.

Action Steps:

» Be open to possibility and partnerships from those who seek you out.

» Keep an eye on what your competitors are doing.

» Maintain healthy relationships with people in similar companies.

» Look for ways to maximize your existing sources of web traffic and bring in new customers.

RULE 40

You Are Never Finished

Building a business from scratch is not like a construction project that will be completed after the paint dries and all of the fixtures have been put in place. There will never be a point when the work of building your business is done. Your business is a living organism that must be cared for and nurtured until it is no longer yours.

Growing and Shrinking Businesses

There are only two types of businesses: growing businesses and shrinking businesses. Businesses never just keep going at their current level of revenue. Regardless of how much current success you have, you need to keep working to grow your business until you sell it or shut it down. If you continue to work on your business, it will continue to grow. If you stop working on your business and start coasting, it will naturally decay over time. Customers will wander off. A competitor will catch up to you. Revenue will decline. Your systems will break down. If you coast for long enough, eventually you will not have much of a business left. Once you have had a significant amount of success in your business, it will be very tempting to take time off to enjoy the stream of revenue that you created and neglect the work it takes to continue growing. Avoid this temptation at all costs.

Regular Re-Evaluation

After you have made it to the point where you can say you have a successful business, take the time to regularly re-evaluate each component. Do a classic SWOT analysis to identify the strengths, weaknesses, opportunities and threats that exist for every part of your business. Consider what aspects of your product, marketing, sales, operations, technical infrastructure, customer service and accounting need shoring up, repair, or restructuring. Identify the strengths and opportunities you have and plan how to capitalize on them. Understand what your business's weak points are and who is out to eat your lunch. By regularly evaluating the different components of your business through a SWOT analysis, the tasks that you need to complete to continue your growth will become clear. Once you have identified an area that you need to focus on, sprint, don't jog, from one task to another and get that part of your business where it needs to be. It's okay to take breaks between sprints, but you need to keep working on your business regardless of how much success you are currently enjoying.

Shifting Strategies

As your business gets larger, the strategies that you will need to use to grow your business will have to change. You cannot expect to build a six-figure business using the same strategies that grew your business to five-figures. You can build a five-figure business doing everything yourself, having no written goals or systems in place. It is impossible to do ten times the amount of work by yourself in order to make ten times the amount of money you are currently making. In order to move from having a five-figure business to a six-figure business, you need to understand your business's core competencies and identify the key tasks that cause your business to generate revenue. As you figure out how to capitalize on those revenue streams, you will need to hire part-time team members and create or purchase software to grow to the six-figure mark. In order to reach the seven-figure mark, you will need to systematize all aspects of your business and have full-time team members run the day-to-day operations so that you can focus solely on growing your business. You will only be able to get to the next tier of income generation by changing your strategies, systematizing your business, delegating day-to-day tasks to team members and using automation where possible. Decide how far you want your business to go, and then make it happen.

Understand your core competencies and identify the key tasks that generate revenue.

Action Steps:

» Work to grow your business or it will begin to shrink.

» Regularly conduct SWOT analysis for all parts of your business.

» Recognize that your strategies need to change to level-up your company's revenue.

Final Thoughts

These 40 rules you have just read are designed to help you avoid many of the mistakes that I have made while building my Internet businesses while maximize the potential for revenue growth that your Internet business can generate. Consider these rules baseline recommendations for running your own business. All of my advice for each rule has come from my personal experiences while building my Internet businesses: American Banking and Market News, Analyst Ratings Network, Lightning Releases and GoGo Photo Contest.

While I run a profitable online company today, I made a lot of mistakes along the way. I paid for things I should never have purchased, signed up for bad business deals, messed up product launches, and created business units that have never gotten off the ground. I learned a lot of lessons from the successes and failures of my businesses during the last eight years and my hope is that you will learn what you need to capitalize on some of my ideas throughout this book. This is not the one and only book on the market about building an internet business. As an entrepreneur, it should be in the pile of books on your desk, by your laptop or on your bookshelf for you to read and reread when you need more information. Use the rules as a scaffold to help you get to the next step in your own business. Building any business from the ground up is not easy, but if you are up for the challenge, the rewards on the other side are hard to beat. Best of luck to you on your journey.

APPENDIX A

Recommended Books and Podcasts

Recommended Books

I have read more than 300 business and leadership books since 2008. The books listed below have provided immeasurable value and education as I have built my Internet businesses. To view a list of the most recent books that I am reading, visit *www.mattpaulson.com/latestbooks*.

- » *The 4-Hour Workweek* by Timothy Ferris
- » *The $100 Startup* by Chris Guillebeau
- » *Built to Sell* by John Warrillow
- » *Business Brilliant* By Lewis Schiff
- » *Cashflow Quadrant* by Robert Kiyosaki
- » *The Compound Effect* by Darren Hardy
- » *Delivering Happiness* by Tony Hsieh
- » *The E-Myth Revisited* by Michael Gerber
- » *EntreLeadership* by Dave Ramsey
- » *The Eventual Millionaire* by Jaime Tardy
- » *Free* by Chris Anderson
- » *How to Get Rich* by Felix Dennis
- » *Internet Prophets* by Steve Olsher
- » *The Lean Startup* by Eric Ries
- » *Lean Startup Marketing* by Sean Ellis
- » *Mastering the Rockefeller Habits* by Verne Harnish
- » *Millionaire Fastlane* by MJ DeMarco
- » *Multiple Streams of Income* by Robert Allen
- » *Necessary Endings* by Henry Cloud
- » *Never Eat Alone* by Keith Ferrazzi and Tahl Raz
- » *The Personal MBA* by Josh Kaufman
- » *Secrets of the Millionaire Mind* by T. Harv Eker
- » *Sell More Software* by Patrick McKenzie

- *Start With Why* by Simon Sinek
- *Start Your Own Business* by Entrepreneur Magazine
- *Street Smarts* by Norm Brodsky and Bo Burlingham
- *The Toilet Paper Entrepreneur* by Mike Michalowicz
- *Tribes* by Seth Godin
- *Work the System* by Sam Carpenter

Recommended Podcasts

Below you will find a list of entrepreneurial podcasts that I subscribe to and listen to on a regular basis. These podcasts provide a significant amount of education and value to online entrepreneurs. I recommend that you subscribe to them as well. To view the most recent list of podcasts that I am listening to, visit *www.mattpaulson.com/latestpodcasts*.

- *48 Days* with Dan Miller (www.48days.com)
- *Bootstrapped with Kids* with Brecht Palombo and Scott Yewell (www.bootstrappedwithkids.com)
- *Build My Online Store* with Terry Lin (www.buildmyonlinestore.com)
- *Email Marketing Podcast* with John McIntyre (www.themcmethod.com)
- *Empire Flippers* with Justin Cooke and Joe Magnotti (www.empireflippers.com)
- *Entrepreneur Showdown* with Joe Cassandra and Dan Franks (www.entrepreneurshowdown.com)
- *Entrepreneur on Fire* with John Lee Dumas (www.entrepreneuronfire.com)
- *Eventual Millionaire* with Jaime Tardy (www.eventualmillionaire.com)
- *Internet Business Mastery* with Jeremy "Sterling" Frandsen and Jason "Jay" Van Orden (www.Internetbusinessmastery.com)
- *Kalzumeus Podcast* with Patrick McKenzie (www.kalzumeus.com/category/podcasts/)
- *Love Your Leap* with John Lee Dumas and Tim Paige (www.loveyourleap.com)
- *Marketing for Founders* with Tim Conley and Jack Zerby

(www.marketingforfounders.com)

- *Marketing Over Coffee* with Christopher Penn and John Wall (www.marketingovercoffee.com)
- *New Business Podcast* with Chris Ducker (www.chrisducker.com)
- *Quit!* with Dan Benjamin and Haddie Cooke (www.5by5.tv/quit)
- *Smart Passive Income* with Pat Flynn (www.smartpassiveincome.com)
- *Startups for the Rest of Us* with Mike Taber and Rob Walling (www.startupsfortherestofus.com)
- *Super Fast Business* with James Schramko (www.superfastbusiness.com)
- This Week in Internet Business (www. thisweekininternetbusiness.com)
- *Tropical MBA* with Dan Andrews and Ian Schoen (www.tropicalmba.com)

APPENDIX B

40 Online Business Ideas

If you have not settled on an idea for your Internet business yet and need some inspiration, here are forty different online business ideas that you could pursue:

- » Create a jobs website for a niche industry and charge for job postings.
- » Write an e-book on a subject that you are knowledgeable about and publish it on Amazon and iBooks.
- » Create a freemium WordPress plug-in.
- » Build a niche e-commerce store that targets people with a specific hobby, such as fishing.
- » Offer freelance writing or press release services.
- » Create themes and sell them through a service like ThemeForest.
- » Build an online membership community around a specific subject or interest.
- » Use email marketing and social media to promote other people's products through affiliate marketing programs.
- » Offer coaching services using any specialized knowledge or skills that you might have.
- » Build niche content websites around specific topics and generate revenue through ad-clicks and affiliate links.
- » Create an online course on subject matter where you have specialized knowledge and experience.
- » Create a software-as-a-service product to solve a problem that a specific industry has.
- » Buy under-priced items at garage sales and sell them on eBay.
- » Offer productized consulting services in which you perform a specific task for a set fee.

- Offer social media management services to small businesses.
- Provide translation services to clients.
- Offer research services in specialized areas like genealogy.
- Create custom web-forms for companies using tools like Wufoo.
- Create resumes and cover letters.
- Provide remote technical support to users with computer problems.
- Sell your photos through stock photography websites.
- Create content on YouTube to build an audience and generate ad-revenue.
- Build a paid smartphone app.
- Provide transcription services for audio content.
- Offer to edit podcasts as a service.
- Sell art and hand-made crafts on Etsy or eBay.
- Create a service to connect entrepreneurs with virtual assistants.
- Set up web software such as WordPress for clients.
- Create professional marketing videos for local companies.
- Purchase expiring domain names and resell them to other companies.
- Create a paid email newsletter.
- Find contract work as a professional blogger through the ProBlogger Job Board.
- Offer ghost-writing services to busy authors.
- Provide marketing services to professionals such as chiropractors or dentists.
- Offer life coaching services through Skype or Google Hangouts.
- Provide proofreading services to authors and bloggers.
- Help companies offer online surveys and collect feedback from their customers.
- Create digital scrap-books and photo albums for busy moms.
- Provide online training for a piece of specialized software.
- Set up Google AdWords campaigns for companies.

Granted, none of these are particularly original, unique or even necessarily good ideas for you. I am not recommending that you should or should not pursue any of the forty ideas listed above. Hopefully they will get you thinking about what businesses you could start using your unique set of talents and abilities. The best idea for you to pursue will not come from a list, a book, or an online course. The business you should pursue will come from your own mind as a result of your knowledge, your research, your experience and your conversations with potential customers.

Thanks

Thank you for purchasing *40 Rules for Internet Business Success* and taking the time to read it. Reading a nonfiction book can take quite a bit of time. Thank you for choosing to spend some of your valuable reading time with my book.

If you would like to share your thanks for this book, the best thing you can do is tell a friend about *40 Rules for Internet Business Success* or buy them a copy. I wrote this book in a small bedroom in my house that I converted to an office. I do not have a major publisher or any outside financial backing for this project. The proceeds from every copy sold goes to help my wife, Karine, and I raise our son and pay for his college education.

You can also show your appreciation for this book by leaving a review where you bought it. To leave a review on Amazon, visit the Amazon product page at *www.mattpaulson.com/amazon*. Please be honest with your review and how this book has or has not helped you on your path to building an Internet business. I want everyone to know how or if this book has changed your life in any significant way.

You can follow me online at my personal blog, www.mattpaulson.com. You can also follow me on twitter (@MatthewDP). If we have met in real life, we can be friends on Facebook (www.facebook.com/MatthewPaulson). If we have not met in real life, you are still welcome to "follow" me on Facebook. I am also on LinkedIn (www.linkedin.com/in/matthewpaulson) and AngelList (www.angel.co/MatthewPaulson). If you would like to hear me talk about various topics, feel free to check out the interviews I have done at *www.mattpaulson.com/interviews*.

Thanks Again and God Bless,

Matthew Paulson
July 21st, 2014
American Consumer News, LLC
Sioux Falls, South Dakota

Acknowledgements

I would like to express my sincere gratitude to my many friends, family members and business acquaintances who have encouraged me while I have built American Consumer News, LLC during the last eight years.

I would like to thank my wife Karine for being incredibly supportive, putting up with my unusual work schedule and trusting me to provide for our family through my business.

I would like to thank my team members including David Anicetti, Donna Helling, Don Miller, Jason Shea, Stevie Shea and Toi Williams. Without them, American Consumer News, LLC, would not be the company that it is today.

Finally, I would like to express my gratitude to Andy Traub and John Meyer who have made this book possible. I would like to thank John for connecting me to other entrepreneurs and showing me that writing a book is not an impossible task through those connections. I would like to thank Andy for coaching me and encouraging me while I wrote this book.

About the Author

Matthew Paulson is entrepreneurial to a fault. Through his company, American Consumer News, LLC, he has built a conglomerate of successful Internet businesses including:

- American Banking & Market News (www.americanbankingnews.com)
- Analyst Ratings Network (www.analystratings.net)
- GoGo Photo Contest (www.gogophotocontest.com)
- Lightning Releases (www.lightningreleases.com)
- Video County (www.videocounty.com)

Matthew holds a B.S. in Computer Science and a M.S. in Information Systems from Dakota State University. He also holds an M.A. in Christian Leadership from Sioux Falls Seminary.

Although he is no stranger to writing, *40 Rules for Internet Business Success* is Matthew's first book and is the culmination of eight years of building Internet businesses.

Matthew resides in Sioux Falls, South Dakota, with his wonderful wife, Karine, and his adorable son, Micah.

Connect with Matthew at:

Matthew's Personal Blog - www.mattpaulson.com
AngelList - www.angel.co/matthewpaulson
Facebook - www.facebook.com/MatthewPaulson
LinkedIn - www.linkedin.com/in/matthewpaulson
Twitter - www.twitter.com/matthewdp
Email - matt@mattpaulson.com

29490213R00116

Printed in Great Britain
by Amazon